GRIMSHAW

Blue

02

SYSTEMS AND STRUCTURE

Blue 02

Introduction: Learning from Nature
Andrew Whalley
6

SYSTEMS

Cooling with Sunlight   British Pavilion for Expo '92   13
Sir Nicholas Grimshaw

Harvesting the Sun   Leaf House   21
Andrew Whalley

Sculpted by the Wind   Southern Cross Station   29
Neil Stonell

The North Face   Adaptive re-use   39
Keith Brewis

Circulation Strategies   The St Botolph Building   49
Ewan Jones

STRUCTURE

Surfaces as Structures
Chris Crombie

Pulkovo Airport 63

Folded Plate Structures
Christian Hönigschmid and Michael Blancato

Horno³: Museo Del Acero 73

Doing More with Less
Paulo Faria and Michael Stein

Fulton Street Transit Centre
Coney Island 85

Core Values
Jolyon Brewis

Eden Project: The Core 97

The Collaborative Process – Grimshaw and Haring
Andrew Thomas

100

Sourcing a Complex Timber Structure
Jerry Tate

102

Learning from Nature

An Introduction to Blue 02 by **Andrew Whalley**

Following a very positive response to our first edition of Blue that explored themes on Waste, Water and Energy, our second volume explores the two complimentary themes of Systems and Structure. The opening essay, by Sir Nicholas Grimshaw, revisits one of our defining projects, the British Pavilion for the World Expo in Seville. Informed by nature, the pavilion used abundant sunshine to solve a problem, creating a cool oasis in Europe's hottest city. It was not only a pioneering demonstration on how technology can be harnessed to resolve environmental challenges but also reveals how we can learn important lessons from regional architectural responses. The region has for generations used fabrics to shade streets and water in fountains and pools to create microclimates. This was a step development in our thinking on architectural responses, harnessing our interest in tectonic solutions with an understanding of natural systems for a truly performative driven design.

I have been fortunate to spend time exploring the Amazonian rainforest with the eminent biologist writer David Campbell, undertaking client research. As David and I explored the rainforest, he pointed out that an architect could have no greater teacher than nature. Nowhere is this more evident than in the Amazon region; after nearly four billion years of life on earth, the area is at its zenith of biodiversity. Though one of the richest ecosystems on the planet, we are only now beginning to understand the richness of plant and animal species where incredibly varied constituents survive on just a few inches of sandy soil, containing few nutrients. The rainforest thrives despite such scant resources through ruthless efficiency and cunning ingenuity: for every problem it invents a solution. With the challenges ahead, posed by our rapid depletion of the world's natural resources, it is hard to imagine a more hopeful model.

Responding to this lesson, and exploring biomimicry, we reinterpreted 'Bicton Glasshouse,' the pioneering Victorian hot house built in Devon,

01

England, with a 21st century version, taking the concept of roof as environmental moderator to the next step in its evolution. Reinterpreted in the form of an architectural leaf harvesting the energy of the sun, with its own interpretation of photosynthesis and like a tree using transpiration, it stores this energy for reuse as the seasons change. However, this performative response to architecture is much broader than energy use and affects all aspects of design, seeking efficiencies with optimum solutions.

In *Circulation Strategies*, Ewan Jones explores a new approach to the vertical movement of people in the St Botolph office building in London. An innovative approach with two separate lifts occupying each lift shaft radically reduces the size of the lift core, making a more efficient building, both in area and its daily operation. An essay by Keith Brewis again utilises this approach, exploring the adaptive re-use of existing office buildings. Instead of tearing down and rebuilding, the addition of an inhabited climatic façade will instead allow our building stock from 40 years ago to be given a new lease of life, with modern high quality working environments that

02

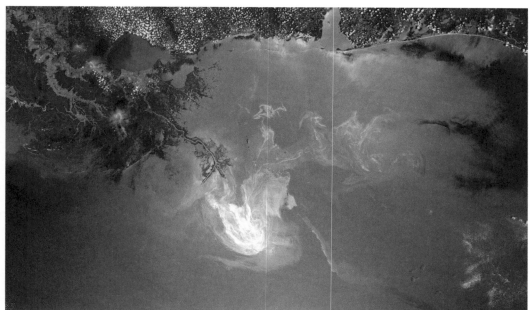

AS DAVID AND I EXPLORED THE RAINFOREST, HE POINTED OUT THAT AN ARCHITECT COULD HAVE NO GREATER TEACHER THAN NATURE

build upon our existing building stock, an approach that was the norm until a generation ago.

In the section on structures, a series of essays investigates projects that we are currently developing using folded plates to create both large and small-scale buildings, an exploration in origami with steel. One of nature's most efficient formations, the spider web, is the inspiration and framework for two very efficient designs in New York, the new Fulton Street Transit Center in lower Manhattan and a 8,000 seat performance arena in Coney Island, Brooklyn.

In a recent interview for *The Guardian* the pre-eminent writer James Lovelock described his despair following the failure of the United Nations summit in Copenhagen. Lovelock questioned our global resolve and ability to act collectively in order to halt the destruction of the planet's current ecosystem through global warming. A sad reflection on humanity, it has taken an environmental disaster of tragic proportions, the oil spill in the Gulf of Mexico, to finally galvanise a broader call for serious investment towards a new approach for a replacement to fossil fuels. As architects, I suppose we should feel somewhat hypocritical discussing sustainability. After all, we lead an industry which consumes half of the world's resources, and then, in the United States, squanders almost three-quarters of the annual energy production — almost all of which is supplied by dwindling and hazardous carbon-based fuels.

While we may feel guilty that our profession carries some of the responsibility for creating this all-consuming built environment, we are also the ones that can help to put it right. ⑧

SECTION ONE
SYSTEMS

What if humans des
systems that celebr
of human creativity,
productivity? That a
safe, our species lea
footprint to delight in

igned products and
ate an abundance
culture, and
re so intelligent and
ves an ecological
, not lament?

William McDonough and Michael Braungart
Cradle to Cradle: Remaking the Way We Make Things

Using the heat of the sun to create an oasis of cool in the hottest city in Spain, the design of the British Pavilion reinterpreted aspects of the local building vernacular.

British Pavilion for Expo '92
Seville, Spain

COOLING WITH SUNLIGHT

Sir Nicholas Grimshaw CBE PRA
Chairman

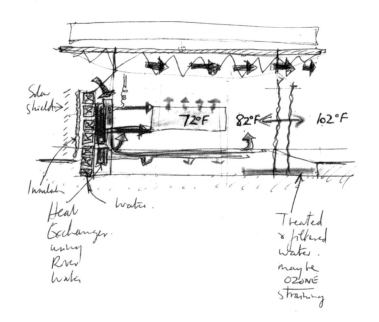

01

With green issues all the rage, I am reminded of our project for the British Pavilion at Expo '92 in Seville. We won the competition 20 years ago and subjected ourselves to a period of enormous excitement and celebration.

The competition concept was entirely based on a response to the climate in Seville which, as Spain's hottest city, was known as "the frying pan of Europe". We thought that we should recognise that people had being living there quite happily for centuries without the huge expense of cooling systems and air-conditioning. We resolved to find out how they had managed.

We quickly saw that the massive masonry walls of the older buildings played an important part in modifying the huge variation in temperature from night time to day time. We also saw that air movement was carefully contrived by having large doorways leading into small courtyards so that cool air from the narrow shaded streets was drawn up through the courtyard and out of the open top. A third factor was the use of water – not just the apparent cooling effect of a small fountain in each courtyard surrounded by plants and ferns, but also the psychological effect of having running water.

The aim for our design was to try to make life bearable for the visitors to the Expo which needed to be held at the hottest time of the year. However, we also wanted to do this with modern materials and, most importantly, using the minimum amount of energy.

The first priority seemed to be to block the very strong afternoon sun, as our site was on the Western perimeter. We did this by using a stack of standard storage tanks filled with water to provide the necessary inertia. Next we determined to 'shield' the building so that no direct sunlight fell on it. We did this with fabric louvres on the roof and the end walls. Finally, we added what was to become the key design feature of the building. This was a 70' x 200' 'water wall'. Solar panels between the fabric

THE AIM FOR OUR DESIGN WAS TO TRY TO MAKE LIFE BEARABLE FOR THE VISITORS TO THE EXPO WHICH NEEDED TO BE HELD AT THE HOTTEST TIME OF THE YEAR

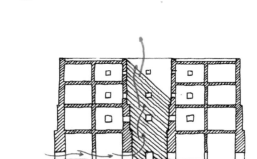

02

01 CONCEPT SKETCH BY NICK GRIMSHAW EXPLAINING HIS VISION OF THE PAVILION AS A MODERATOR OF CLIMATE
02 TRADITIONAL BUILDINGS IN HOT CLIMATES USE THE 'CHIMNEY EFFECT' TO CAUSE AIR MOVEMENT FROM COOL NARROW STREETS WHILE HEAVY MASONRY HAS THE ABILITY TO STABILISE TEMPERATURE
03 THE 'WATER WALL' ON THE BUILDING'S EAST SIDE WAS A MAJOR COOLING ELEMENT
04 CANOPIES SHADE A STREET IN SEVILLE
05 WATER FEATURE IN THE ALHAMBRA PALACE IN GRANADA

03

04

05

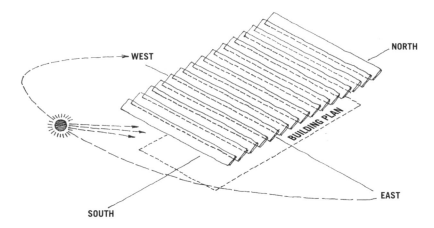

WEST

NORTH

BUILDING PLAN

EAST

SOUTH

05

05 ARRAYS OF SOLAR CELLS SHADE
    THE ROOF FROM DIRECT
    SUNLIGHT AND PROVIDE POWER
    FOR THE BUILDING
06 COOLING OF THE SOUTH
    ELEVATION WAS ACHIEVED BY
    EXTERNAL SHADING DEVICES
07 WITHIN THE PAVILION'S
    'CATHDRAL LIKE' DOMINANT
    SPACE THE AIR TEMPERATURE
    WAS COOLED BY UP TO 10° C
    ON THE HOTTEST DAYS WHEN
    EXTERNAL AIR TEMPERATURE
    CAN REACH 45 DEGREES

PARADOXICALLY, THE HEAT OF THE SUN PROVIDES THE COOLING FOR THE BUILDING

roof screens provided power for pumps to push water to a channel at the top of the building. Water was allowed to run from this channel down the face of the glazed façade. This created a wonderful patterned waterfall effect which greatly intrigued queuing visitors.

As this wall faced east (meaning that it was rapidly in the shade), it had the effect of cooling down the whole building. The building became famous for being a cool oasis for visitors. They also benefited from the longest bar on the Expo site which supplied them with (surprisingly cool) British beer.

We won the prize for the least energy used by any of the 106 National Pavilions on the Expo site and I believe that this project kindled the great interest in energy and sustainability that the Grimshaw office has pursued ever since. Ⓑ

06

07

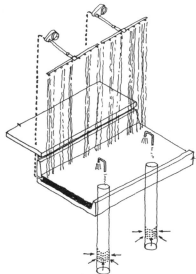

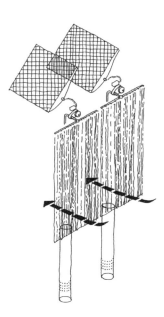

08 THE BUILDING'S MAIN COOLING ELEMENT, THE 'WATER WALL', IS SUPPLIED BY BOREHOLES PROVIDING COOL WATER WHICH IS THEN LIFTED TO THE TOP OF THE FAÇADE BY PUMPS

09 SOLAR POWER IS USED TO RUN THE PUMPS OPERATING THE 'WATER WALL'. THUS THE HEAT OF THE SUN PROVIDES THE COOLING FOR THE BUILDING

05 AFTER THE EXPO THE PAVILION'S SOLAR CELLS (A), PUMPS (B) AND CONTAINERS (C) WERE USED TO PROVIDE BASIC WATER SUPPLIES FOR THE THIRD WORLD

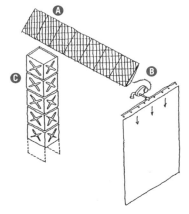

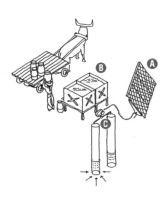

To be natural, a human like a plant or a tree. Th houses and cities toget animals should be a na effect buildings should nature but that man an should be an inseparab

product need not look
e great aim is that
her with plants and
tural biotop, that in
not be directed against
d his technology
le part of nature.

Frei Otto
Natural Constructions

We designed a roof that was a technological interpretation of photosynthesis, harvesting sunlight in the summer, using some of the energy to run the environmental systems and storing the remainder, to be drawn on in the depth of winter.

Leaf House

HARVESTING THE SUN

Andrew Whalley
Managing Partner

01

Almost all of the earth's energy is derived from the sun; this energy is almost exclusively harvested by the unique ability of plants to convert the sun's energy through photosynthesis. This process supplies humans with their vital support systems of oxygen, food, fuel, medicine and clothes. Even fossil fuels are the results of photosynthesis from millions of years ago. Our civilisation and our potential as human beings is inexorably and unavoidably entwined with developments in science, travel and plant exploitation. This scientific journey bloomed in the 19th century and, coupled with the impact of the industrial revolution, was the catalyst for a new type of architecture – the glasshouse.

Glasshouse design has been a constant inspiration for architects and engineers. A new approach to creating highly efficient transparent structures was inspired and influenced by two Scotsmen, Sir George Mackenzie and John Claudius Loudon. Mackenzie developed the curved glass house geometry that ran 'parallel to the vaulted surface of the heavens', tracking the sun for maximum gain of heat and light. Loudon patented the technique of utilising the malleable qualities of wrought iron, with curved sash bars that allowed bell shape and dome geometries. These new ideas – developed as a technological solution to creating artificial environments – went on to ignite a new approach to architecture and construction.

We wanted to rethink the 'glass' house as a true 'green' house, drawing on the analogy of a leaf and photosynthesis. To us this meant not just capturing heat and light but harvesting and storing and using it, just like trees which capture the sun's energy in its leaves through photosynthesis and proceeds to move and store the resource through transpiration. Our Leaf House was designed for a northern hemisphere location where the interior would be shaded and cooled from the excess heat of the summer and the captured energy could be used to temper the cold of the winter.

We wanted to follow this analogy into the structure

WE WANTED TO RETHINK THE 'GLASS' HOUSE AS A TRUE 'GREEN' HOUSE, DRAWING ON THE ANALOGY OF A LEAF AND PHOTOSYNTHESIS

02

03

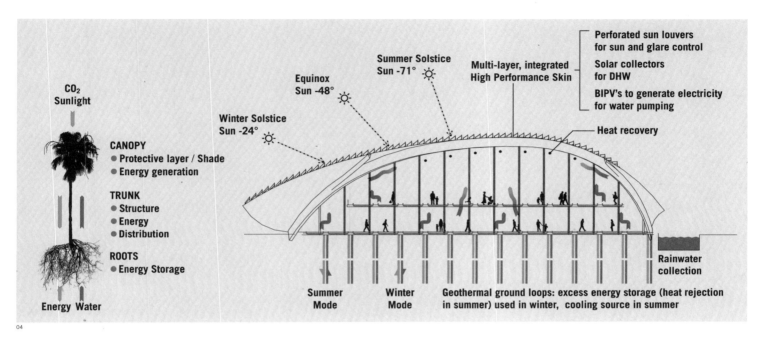

CO₂
Sunlight

CANOPY
● Protective layer / Shade
● Energy generation

TRUNK
● Structure
● Energy
● Distribution

ROOTS
● Energy Storage

Energy Water

Winter Solstice
Sun -24°

Equinox
Sun -48°

Summer Solstice
Sun -71°

Multi-layer, integrated
High Performance Skin

Perforated sun louvers
for sun and glare control

Solar collectors
for DHW

BIPV's to generate electricity
for water pumping

Heat recovery

Summer
Mode

Winter
Mode

Geothermal ground loops: excess energy storage (heat rejection
in summer) used in winter, cooling source in summer

Rainwater
collection

04

01 AN INTERIOR VIEW OF THE LEAF
FORM TIMBER STRUCTURE,
WITH A MINIMAL USE OF STEEL
PLATES AND CABLES TO KEEP
IT AS LIGHT AND TRANSPARENT
AS POSSIBLE
02 BICTON GLASS HOUSE, DEVON
PIONEERED THE INNOVATIVE
COMBINATION OF WROUGHT IRON
AND GLASS AS DOMED SHELL
03 VACUUM SOLAR COLLECTORS
ARE UP TO 80% EFFICIENT IN
CONVERTING THE HEAT FROM
THE SUN INTO USABLE ENERGY,
WORKING EVEN ON COLD BUT
SUNNY WINTER DAYS
04 THE ROOF ACTS LIKE A LEAF,
HARVESTING SUNLIGHT
WITH ITS ARRAY OF VACUUM
SOLAR COLLECTORS. THE
ENVIRONMENTAL SYSTEM
WORKS IN THE SAME WAY AS
'TRANSPIRATION' IN A PLANT;
ITALICISING THE ENERGY TO
RUN ITS SYSTEMS AND STORING
EXCESS ENERGY IN THE GROUND
FOR REUSE IN THE WINTER
05 THE BUILDING IS SHADED BY
THE 'LEAF BLADES' ARRAYS
OF SOLAR COLLECTORS AND
PHOTOVOLTAICS

05

and use renewable materials where possible. The structure is therefore made from wood gluelams with the minimal use of steel to keep it as light and transparent as possible. Inspired by aircraft design, the roof structure borrows from a timber and cable spanned aircraft wing, but with the geometry of a leaf. The central stem is made with timber arches and of this stem, bow-string trusses arch to the ground.

Like the cellulose structure of a leaf, we saw the roof structure as the means of supporting our 'chlorophyll' environmental control system: a number of layers that could both shade the interior and harvest the sun.

In translating these elements, our approach is to emulate the life systems of plants and to blend technology and nature in an expressive, meaningful and bold architecture.

The Leaf House was optimised in every orientation to gather the sun's energy, dispersing some of the energy for immediate use in various building functions and storing the rest for future use in other seasons.

We were particularly inspired by the leaf of the Carnauba tree. The complex nature of the Carnauba leaf – with its ability to secrete wax through its leaves, apparently in defense against the hot winds and droughts of its native habitat – provides endless inspiration for developing a structure that also relies on its efficient and dynamic components to be self-sustaining and which can adapt itself to the environment. During the photosynthesis process chlorophyll, the green pigment in leaves, transforms the sun's unusable sunlight energy into chemical energy to produce sugar (fuel/energy).

Six molecules of water and six molecules of CO_2 produce one molecule of sugar and six molecules of oxygen:

$$6H_2O + 6CO_2 \longrightarrow C_6H_{12}O_6 + 6O_2$$

The leaf acts as the solar collector. The raw materials plants use for the process are water and CO_2. The vehicle for the circulation of raw materials is the veins (xylem cells). The by-product of the process is sugar (energy) and oxygen. The energy is stored in the roots.

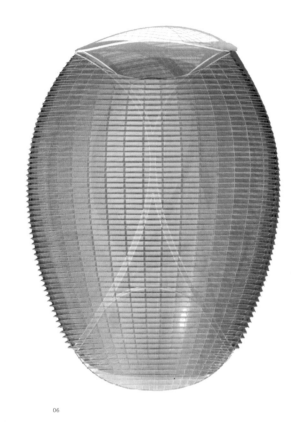

06

06 THE SHIELDING LEAF BLADES OVER THE ENTIRE ROOF ARE IN TURN COMPRISED OF CIRCULAR GLASS TUBES TO MAXIMISE THE SOLAR COLLECTING SURFACE

07 THE BUILDING ENCLOSURE COMPRISES OF A SERIES OF LAYERS, A TIMBER AND CABLE STAYED STRUCTURE SUPPORTS A HIGH PERFORMANCE GLASS SKIN PROTECTED FROM THE SUN WITH LAYERS OF SOLAR COLLECTORS, HARVESTING SUNLIGHT AND SHADING THE ENCLOSURE

08 THE SHELL FORM OF THE ROOF IS DESIGNED TO KEEP THE STRUCTURE AS LIGHT AS POSSIBLE BUT STILL USING TIMBER AS A RENEWABLE RESOURCE

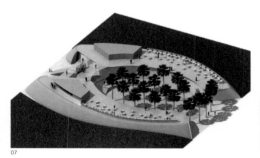

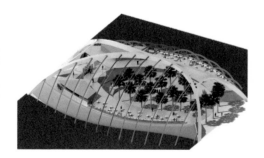

07

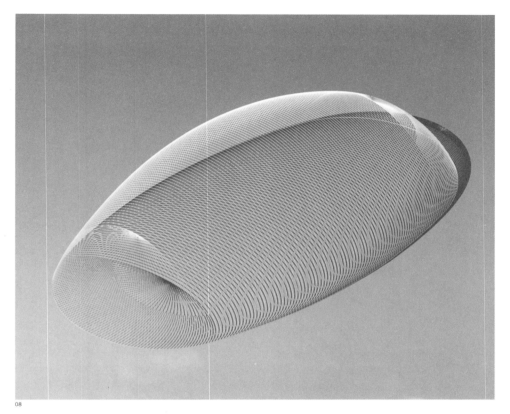

08

OUR INTENTION WAS TO CREATE AN ENCLOSURE THAT DEFINED SPACE AND CONTROLLED ENVIRONMENT THROUGH STRUCTURE AND SKIN

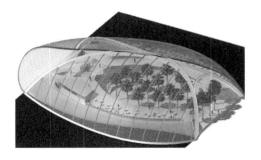 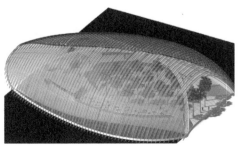

With this process as a starting point, an idea developed – an organic form, natural materials, the sun as energy source, the ground as energy storage, the structure as the channels for transporting energy, water as the conductor:

The heating and cooling of the various spaces would be provided by a closed loop geothermal heat pump system. The geothermal system water would connect to a bank of water-to-water reversible heat pumps located in a central mechanical room. A four-pipe HHW and CHW piping network would distribute heating and cooling to the various air handling units and other heat emitting equipment throughout the facility.

The geothermal system would offer several advantages over a 'typical' boiler and chiller installation:

- The geothermal system has no cooling tower. The geothermal well field, once installed and tested, requires virtually no maintenance.
- Reversible heat pumps generate both heating and cooling using electricity as the primary energy source. The electricity required to run some of the pumps can be offset through the use of building integrated photovoltaics (BIPVs).

During the summer, heat is rejected to the ground through a water-to-water heat exchanger. Cool water is delivered to air handling equipment. Solar shading prevents excess heat gain from increasing the cooling load.

During the winter, heat is extracted from the ground. To increase the heating efficiency, heat from the solar thermal panels could be introduced to the geothermal loop during the heating seasons. The mass of the ground is able to store this heat and allows it to be utilised during the heating season. Solar shading elements will be positioned to allow passive solar heating from low-angle sun in the winter months.

We developed the leaf house structure with Dewhurst McFarlane and the environmental system with Buro Happold; our intention was to create a seamless fusion of engineering and architecture, an enclosure that defined space and controlled environment through structure and skin, just as nature operates. Although a theoretical project, it is a theme that we are continuing to explore. ⓑ

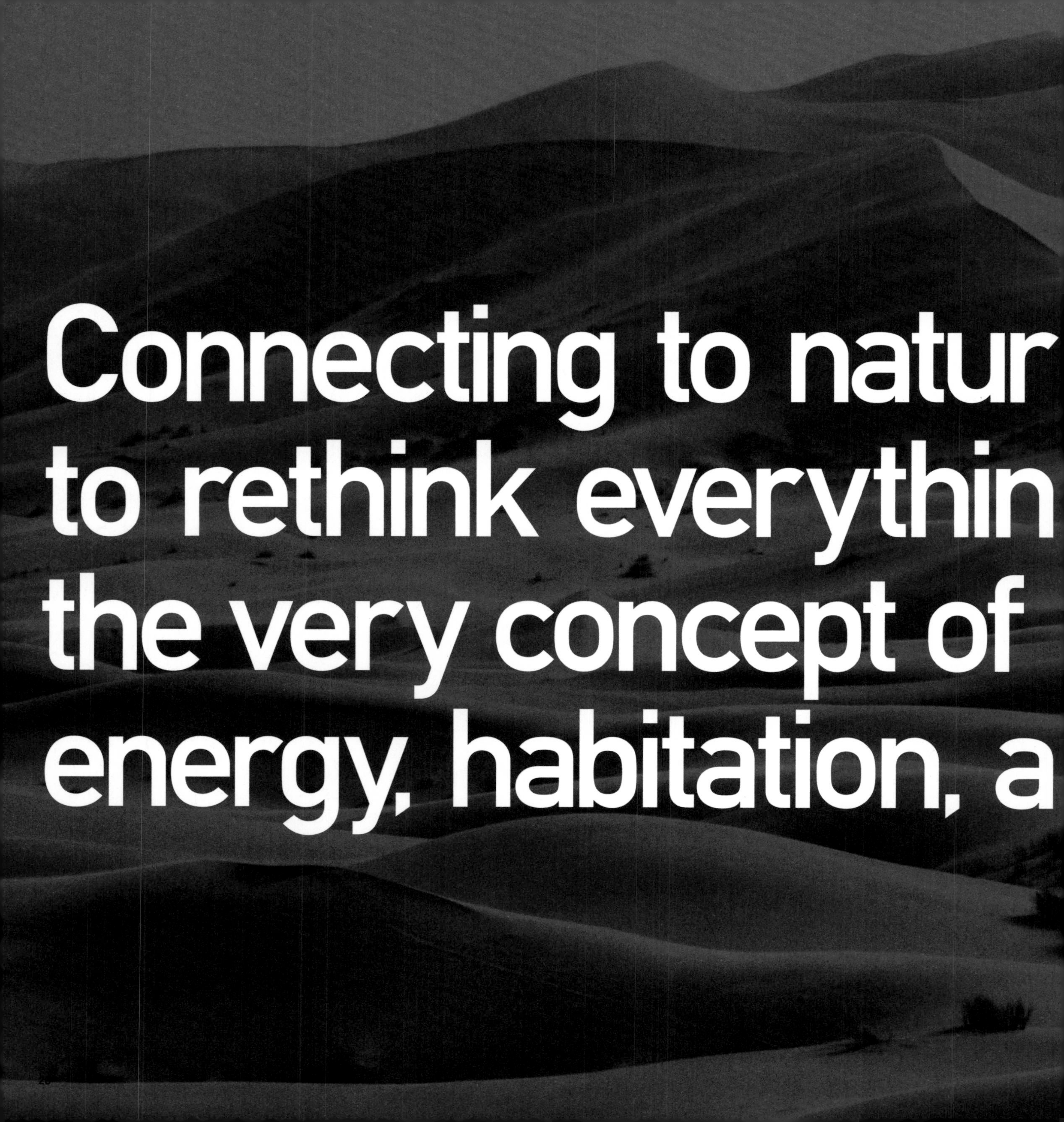

Connecting to natur
to rethink everythin
the very concept of
energy, habitation, a

al flows allows us
g under the sun:
power plants, of
nd transportation.

William McDonough and Michael Braungart
Cradle to Cradle: Remaking the Way We Make Things

Southern Cross Station, with its landmark
roof designed to provide natural ventilation,
aims to promote and deepen environmental
awareness in design.

Southern Cross Station
Melbourne, Australia

SCULPTED
BY THE WIND

Neil Stonell
Partner

Additional material by
Matthew Jessop of Built Ecology

Southern Cross Station is Melbourne's main transport interchange, straddling the edge of the city grid, and the newly regenerated Docklands precinct to the west. In 2001 the Victorian Government created a brief for the redevelopment of the existing Spencer Street Station, a terminus and interchange that was failing to provide the users of the public transport network with an experience appropriate for Victoria's premier station and gateway to the regions. A landmark world-class facility was sought to accommodate the existing 15 million passengers that pass through the station each year and support the projected 35 million per year by 2050.

From the outset, the design team at Grimshaw were acutely aware of the responsibility to meet the aspirations of the public transport user by providing a well-designed interchange, whilst also understanding the need to promote connection between the two disparate precincts on either side of the rail corridor. The new station improves this by lining the three major streets that it bounds, two of which are elevated across the tracks, with pedestrian concourses. Glazed façades allow the inner life of the station – both people and trains – to be exposed to the city from long vistas in most directions. By removing the existing underground concourses and tunnels and providing these street level concourses, the design team were able to introduce airport-style customer information facilities and create a large waiting hall with bars, food outlets and shops spread amongst the more traditional transport services. This is all laid out under a single expansive roof that helps provide the station with a coherent identity and the precinct with a landmark.

Equally important to Grimshaw was the ambition to generate the design from performance driven sustainability principles in parallel to the civic needs. The Government brief, whilst completely pragmatic in its transport and urban aspirations, did not embody any significant environmental agenda, requiring only that the "mechanical, electrical and

hydraulic services of the Facility....minimise energy consumption without compromising the reliability, service delivery and specified accommodation standards". In essence, the brief assumed that the designers would provide a traditional solution using mechanical services to ventilate public areas.

Victoria's railway network continues to use diesel as well as electric engine locomotives. Trains are of different types and have exhaust points either in front-end locomotives or in multiple units along their length. Previous experience had taught us that the collection of diesel fumes in fireproofed ducts above each possible engine location, then filtering and discharging the exhaust, is both obtrusive and highly energy consumptive. These systems demand not only ongoing maintenance and substantial running costs but would also require additional visually intrusive building structure to support such services.

As an alternative the design team proposed that the 36,000 sq m station roof as well as the perimeter façades be designed as a true 'skin' for the station, protecting the inside from wind and rain while allowing it to breathe and 'sweat' – naturally exhausting contaminated air and aiding cooling during the warmer months.

Grimshaw worked closely with Advanced Environmental Concepts (recently renamed Built Ecology) to develop a natural ventilation strategy that would greatly reduce the impact of the station's design on the external environment, lowering greenhouse gas emissions, greatly reducing the station's dependence on carbon dioxide producing energy resources, and reducing plant maintenance. The roof form and detail subsequently evolved as a consequence, emerging not from any architectural agenda but pragmatically and purposefully from these environmental and performance-driven principles. The solution is a reinterpretation of the great historic rail 'sheds' of the nineteenth century, which provided high vaulting internal spaces able to collect rising smoke and steam in the apex of their arches before discharging them high above the station through clear-storey vents.

Continuous arches or barrel-vaulted roof structures similar to those seen in historic station halls, were quickly discounted for use on Southern Cross

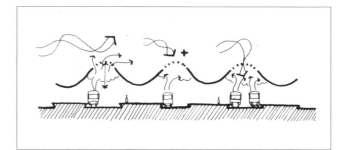

A flat roof plane will trap and hold hot air, contaminates and diesel fumes. The zero pressure differential between inside and out creates internal diesel fume drift.

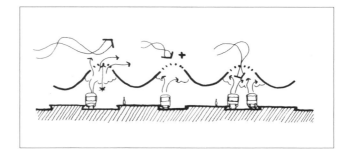

The adoption of a traditional barrel-vaulted solution would prevent lateral fume drift but the high level concourses at Bourke and Collins Streets would become polluted due to longitudinal drift.

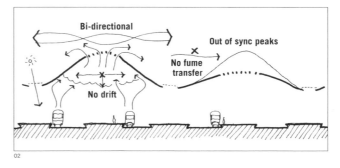

Individual moguls help trap the contaminated air and with the exploitation of the thermal stack effect and the prevailing NW and SW prevailing winds, contaminated air can be extracted naturally.

01　SOUTHERN CROSS STATION'S
　　ICONIC ROOF OVERLOOKED BY
　　MELBOURNE'S HIGHEST BUILDINGS
02　CONCEPT DRAWINGS

EQUALLY IMPORTANT TO GRIMSHAW WAS THE AMBITION TO GENERATE THE DESIGN FROM PERFORMANCE-DRIVEN SUSTAINABILITY PRINCIPLES IN PARALLEL TO THE CIVIC NEEDS

Station due to the proximity of the raised public concourses relative to the roof's springing points at either end of the station. Instead, a series of offset vaulted domes are located above each track bed acting as reservoirs to the rising diesel fumes. At their apex, louvred vents are introduced, designed to maximise air pressure from the seasonal prevailing winds, and through the stack effect help draw the contaminants out of the space. When combined across the site a beautifully seductive undulating blanket is formed – like a desert landscape, or a mogul run.

The station's undulating roof form also contains a cavity between the profiled aluminium top sheet and the soffit panels below. Warm and contaminated air enters this cavity through openings between the soffit panels, meaning that air flow is accelerated, taking advantage of the temperature differential as the space is heated by the external top sheet. This hot air then flows up and out through louvred vents at the apex of each dome.

The station ventilation design was developed through computer simulation techniques that enabled an accurate prediction of the air quality and behaviour within the station supported by best practice environmental design. Thermal Analysis Software and Computational fluid dynamics (CFD) were used to explicitly ascertain the potential for buoyancy ventilation and to calculate the behavioural properties of fluid.

CFD was used extensively to inform the design at all stages. Initially, it was used to demonstrate the merit and the thinking behind a mogul-like roof design. A simple 2D model can show that the wave shapes create areas of negative pressure at the top of the mogul. This model illustrated that local external wind conditions would favourably influence the capacity of natural ventilation exhaust volumes through the moguls with each vent having the potential for air flow rates of between 16,000L/s and 43,500L/s; compared with an alternative mechanical ventilation scheme, which was designed to achieve 15,000L/s.

The design was then taken further to test the indoor air quality of the station whilst diesel locomotives are running. Where bulk air flow analysis shows that the space can relieve heat build-up in the space

03

ULTIMATELY THE ROOF APPEARS TO BE SCULPTED BY THE WIND, MUCH LIKE A SAND DUNE

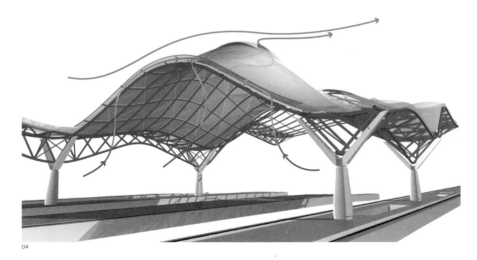

04

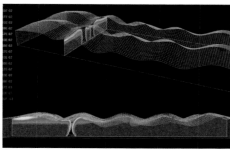

05

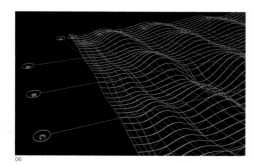

06

07

through the stack effect, the CFD model shows that the temperature and properties of the exhaust alone is enough to drive the ventilation without simulating internal heat loads or solar heat loads that would further assist the ventilation flow rate.

The design also needed to determine a 'worst-case' scenario which was difficult to surmise. This could be a situation where trains are running at full throttle, creating more plentiful exhaust contaminants (however it could be argued that the full throttle scenario also creates extra heat and exhaust flow, thereby artificially enhancing ventilation quantities). Thus two adjacent trains were tested under this full throttle scenario along with a more typical train idling condition. Both events provided acceptable air quality results, with the CFD analysis confirming that the roof geometry would enhance the efficiency of the ventilation and that the passive design not only enables exhaust quantities to be achieved by virtue of the hot exhaust gases but also did not rely on solar gain or internal heat loads.

Using Grimshaw's detailed 3D roof model of the moguls, which vary from 24 metres to 6 metres above the ground plane below, Advanced Environmental were able to assess the complete station geometry, local wind effects on actual ventilation flows, specific removal of train exhaust gases and particulates and determine the necessary apex louvre and façade openings.

03 VIEW ACROSS THE ROOF SHOWING KALZIP ROOF SHEET, SKYLIGHTS AND LOUVRE CAPS TO APEX OF ROOF MOGULS
04 DIAGRAM SHOWING AIR MOVEMENT THROUGH ROOF CAVITY
05 FULL THROTTLE TRAIN SCENARIO PASSIVE SOLUTION
06 MODELLING OF FIRE IN EARLY STAGES OF DEVELOPMENT
07 DUNES DRIFT ACROSS THE DESERT FLOOR IN QATAR, A LANDSCAPE DEFINED BY INTERACTION WITH THE WIND
08 2D COMPUTATIONAL FLUID DYNAMIC MODEL SHOWING NEGATIVE PRESSURE AT APEX OF MOGULS

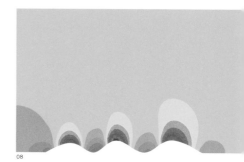

08

CFD modelling enabled the design team to confirm with confidence that air quality standards were met, and predicted that both carbon monoxide and nitrogen dioxide levels complied with standards and health and safety requirements. It was also utilised to assess the design in a fire simulation. The same basic principles apply to the fire scenario as apply to the ventilation of diesel exhaust fumes. A 20 Mega-Watt "ultra-fast" train fire was tested over a time period of 8 minutes using the CFD model, with the results suggesting that the heat from the fire would drive the fire smoke toward the station roof cavity through natural buoyancy.

As well as exhausting contaminated air, the design supports the thermal performance requirements that needed to be met for the space, as the mogul design draws fresh air past the occupants, even on days where there is little or no wind. The roof and façades protect the whole station from wind, rain and excessive direct sun, and help minimise radiant temperatures within the space whilst maintaining the visual transparency through the façades, an important urban response.

Public facilities have been laid out within the station to maximise the benefits provided by the envelope. The concourse waiting areas are located away from the entrances and in general are not enclosed. Where necessary the waiting areas are heated using slab heating systems. Where additional intervention is required to provide an acceptable indoor thermal environment, supplementary heating and cooling is provided. As an example, an enclosed waiting area beneath the Collins St concourse has been provided with a dedicated air-conditioning system, a solution appropriate to such a space. These systems effectively deliver radiant heat to the occupants in an energy efficient way, minimising wasted energy.

The installation of double skin ETFE fabric skylights directly above the platforms provide natural light to the passengers below and the insulating properties of the air within the ETFE pillow protects from excessive radiant heat. A light-diffusing frit has been applied to the skylight fabric, providing a scattering effect to the natural light and reducing the potential for daylight to act as a glare source. This design negates the need to

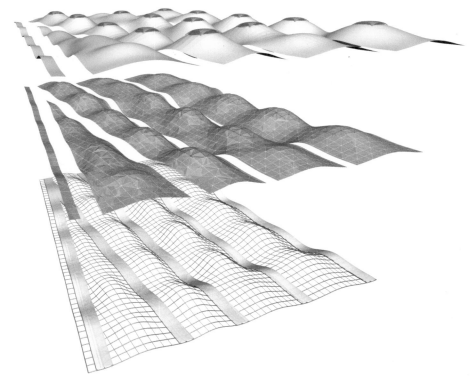

09

operate electric lights during the day which would otherwise be required.

The station remained in operation throughout its redevelopment, even as its roof was being assembled above the platforms. The ventilation solution also had to be functional throughout construction and this relied upon a balancing of free area around the station façades. The delayed completion of the Western façade created imbalance in the free area locations of each façade. This created some performance issues as diesel was not being evacuated as quickly as had been hoped. Thorough testing at that time, and at completion of the façades soon after, proved that the design met, and is exceeding all, performance targets. Roof air quality sensors continue to provide readings for the station operator. Ensuring good quality performance data

is provided throughout the project life, both during and post construction, is essential in a project of such complexity.

The success of the Southern Cross Station project stems from the complete alignment of aspirations within the design team. Working to a shared vision, the complex environmental solution was made easier to achieve. The support given to the design team by the contractor in finding the right design solution was imperative and should not be underestimated. While the roof was designed to ensure that fans could be retrofitted as a fall back scenario, Leighton Contractors allowed the design to adequately develop and be optimised through the early stages of the contract. The performance testing has reconfirmed that there is no need for any additional mechanical plant to aid the

10

THE SUCCESS OF THE PROJECT STEMS FROM THE COMPLETE ALIGNMENT OF ASPIRATIONS WITHIN THE DESIGN TEAM

09 EXPLODED AXONOMETRIC SHOWING ROOF BUILD UP: KALZIP ALUMINIUM SANDWICH PANELS AND SUPPORTING STEEL WORK LATTICE
09 INTERNAL VIEW OF STATION

ventilation of the space.

Grimshaw continue to develop designs that confront the environmental responsibilities of the building and of the site which can often create the architectural form and provide a more responsible building. Southern Cross Station is highly energy efficient in comparison to a traditional building and has fulfilled the aspiration for both lighting and air conditioning tending towards a zero energy consumption. This is important – as energy costs increase, the project must not become a financial burden on the public transport network and take funding away from other transport developments.

The transformation of a maligned urban site into Southern Cross Station was an ambitious attempt to improve the nature of transport architecture and reinstate a level of amenity commensurate with the status of the station, while working to stimulate development throughout the precinct and towards the Docklands. If the station's true architecture is internal, its exterior will become its symbol. The fifth elevation – the rolling landscape of the performative roof, when viewed from the high buildings surrounding it, becomes the beacon for this corner of Melbourne. It also creates a clear statement of intent that such public buildings must be more responsible to the environment in which they sit – both in terms of the civic and the sustainable. Ⓑ

Taking into account demolition, rebuilding, and overall growth, about **50%** of t of he building stock

2050

will consist
of buildings
that exist today.

Steve Burrows of Arup for the Design Futures Council
Survival of the Most Sustainable

How we might transform existing commercial building stock into healthy, productive and efficient places in which to work.

Adaptive re-use

THE
NORTH FACE

Keith Brewis
Managing Partner

Ongoing experiences in the commercial office sector have shown that the traditional 1970s, 1980s and 1990s developer-driven edict of simply seeking to maximise net to gross floor area in the search for the highest yielding property no longer has the same relevance.

Now instead *workplace* practices – how individual office-workers behave, whether alone, in clusters, as teams, as departments, and how each might engage with the other and with their clients or suppliers – has become profoundly important in planning space. The emergence of terms such as *break-out*, *hub*, *winter-garden*, *third space* or *place* pervade and allude to quality not quantity – effectiveness not efficiency. The employee has become more valuable as an asset and their working environment more considered, and with this change has come a wave of buildings that are well-organised spatially. They tend to have adaptable, uninterrupted large floor-plates, serviced by side or multiple cores, and are low to medium rise.

In parallel with this evolution of commercial space, an energy-conscious era is also upon us, with individual buildings planning highly efficient and adaptable ventilation and lighting systems working in tandem with passive and active façades and coupled with sophisticated Building Management Controls.

So where does this leave our existing building stock and what might we do with the huge stock of vertically stacked, small floor-plate high rise buildings planned around very tightly constrained central cores?

For decades many high-rise towers were erected around the world with little regard for energy consumption. The implementation of passive systems within many of these towers was almost unheard of and at the time of their inception would most likely have been ridiculed. Many towers conceived at this time did not even

employ double glazing to their façades, and while electricity was cheap and abundant, there was little or no consideration of carbon emissions, or life-cycle cost.Both were ignored or left unconsidered for the benefit of minimising capital expenditure at the time of construction, to maximise the developer's immediate profit.

Within developed societies we are now acknowledging that our current building stock is too inefficient to sustain, and yet it is also now too large a problem to ignore.

ON AVERAGE, THE COMMERCIAL SECTOR ACCOUNTS FOR
48%
OF (A CITY'S) EMISSIONS

THIS FIGURE IS DOMINATED BY AIR-CONDITIONING, AND LIGHTING SYSTEMS, WHICH TOGETHER ACCOUNT FOR

84%
ON AVERAGE, OF THE TOTAL ENERGY USE

Source: City of Melbourne's
1200 buildings report

"80 billion British Thermal Units of energy are embodied in a typical 50,000 square foot commercial building, the equivalent of 640,000 gallons of gasoline.

A commercial building of this size releases about the same amount of carbon into the atmosphere as driving a car 2.8 million miles. Demolishing it creates nearly 4,000 tonnes of waste.

Recent research indicates that even if 40% of these materials are recycled, it takes nearly 65 years for a green, efficient new office building to recover the energy lost in demolishing an existing building."

SOURCE: ADVISORY COUNCIL ON HISTORIC PRESERVATION

The argument for retrofitting over demolition should – and will – prove to be irrefutable and with this the focus will turn rapidly to upgrading old buildings.

Our existing building stock presents us with a multitude of common issues, including high heat gain through poor orientation or inadequate façade systems; difficult and inefficient to regulate locally with ageing mechanical systems which themselves are highly energy consumptive; uninhabitable areas immediately adjacent to the northern and north western elevations due to excessive radiant heat; and seriously constrained vertical connection relying solely upon the central core bank of lifts. Additionally, very tight floor-to-floor heights and constrained vertical risers give limited options for the reticulation of primary building services from the core, and only restricted internal planning options are available due to constant and small core to façade depths.

A result of these issues we are witnessing many buildings, which are evidently suitable for retro-fitting, undergoing a re-cladding, often in parallel with mechanical plant replacement or overhaul.

If upgrades to plant and façades are done well then the obvious advantages in not having to demolish a building include the maintaining of embodied energy, the creation of high energy savings at low capital cost, the reduction of carbon output and with it pre-empting the large potential

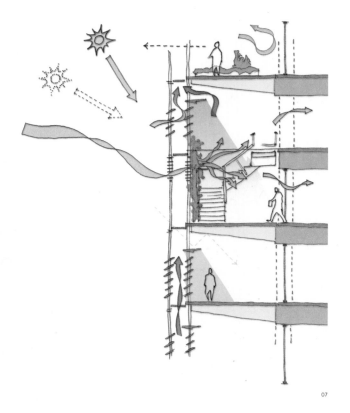

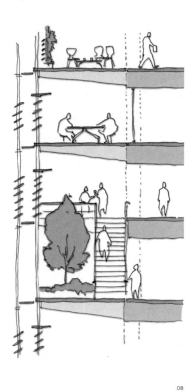

07

08

05

energy cost increases as a result of future emerging carbon taxation.

However, this seems to ignore the other fundamental issues that many central-core high-rise towers have; that they have become unsuitable to many organisations who wish to have inter-departmental links, greater connectedness between departments, greater varied open-planned space, and spaces that are special, and more human.

If owners are spending money sorting out energy consumption, might it not be worth contemplating investing more capital to create additional space with greater flexibility? The argument might be for a new zone rather than just a new skin. As I have been thinking of this while living in the southern hemisphere in Australia I refer to it as the North Face.

While a new skin or façade system, coupled with an upgrade or replacement of the ventilation or cooling systems, will achieve greater energy efficiency, by simultaneously introducing an interstitial floor zone on the north (sunny) façade of a building then this zone can be designed to rectify

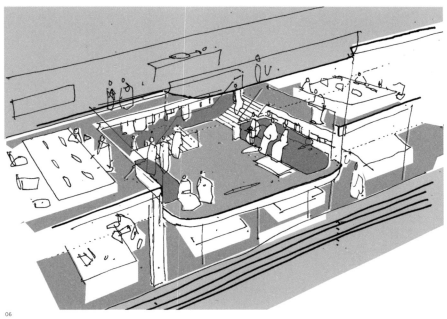

06

MIGHT IT NOT BE WORTH CONTEMPLATING INVESTING MORE CAPITAL TO CREATE ADDITIONAL SPACE WITH GREATER FLEXIBILITY?

03 **SECTION SHOWING NORTH FACE ZONE ACTING AS INTERSTITIAL BUFFER ZONE**
04 **SECTION SHOWING NORTH FACE ZONE PROVIDING COMMUNAL, CONNECTION ZONE**
05 **DIFFERENT DEPARTMENTS AND USES CONNECTED OVER ADJACENT FLOORS**
06 **FLEXIBLE, BREAK-OUT SPACES BEYOND THE ORIGINAL FAÇADE LINE**

issues of light penetration, passive heat and ventilation regulation, services and social inter-connectivity. The opportunity seems to exist to not only improve the energy efficiency of building stock but also to create a more flexible, adaptive and healthier (and therefore more valuable) office space, thus creating a new asset to an old building.

The north face zone might provide an additional five or six metres' depth of space to that frontage, which will give greater flexibility, allowing offices to offer a combination of deep and perimeter space; passively

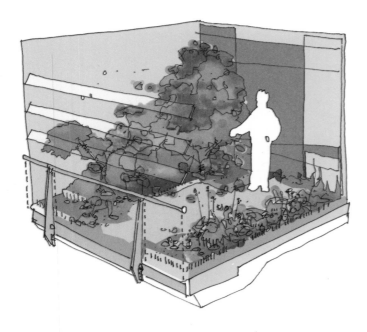

08

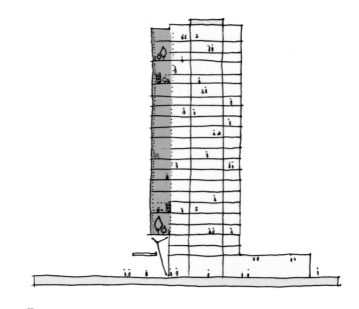

09

THE INCLUSION OF THIS BUFFER ZONE OFFERS THE INTRODUCTION OF SOCIAL, WINTER-GARDEN, MEETING AND WRITE-UP AREAS

reduce radiant heat into the building; save energy by separating the northern zone from the main building; allow greater control of daylight; offer the promotion of social and inter-departmental connection between floors; promote a healthier workplace environment through the introduction of winter-gardens; promote better ventilation air filtration and subsequent reduction of Sick Building syndrome; create a new zone for services reticulation which is peristitial rather than interstitial; and create greater net to gross efficiencies and more adaptable plates.

The inclusion of this buffer zone offers the introduction of social, winter-garden, meeting and write-up areas, as well as the possible interaction between floors through open or fire compartmented staircases that create both dynamic and efficient working environments.

09   **EXTERNAL PROTECTED WINTER-GARDEN**
09   **NORTH FACE ZONE OCCUPYING AIR-RIGHT SPACE OVER PODIUM SET-BACK**
10   **CONSTRUCTION IN PHASES USING EXISTING FAÇADE AS HOARDING LINE**
11   **PLAN INDICATING POTENTIAL FOR SERVICES, STAIRCASES, MEETING ROOMS AND GREEN SPACE TO THE SUNNY FAÇADE**

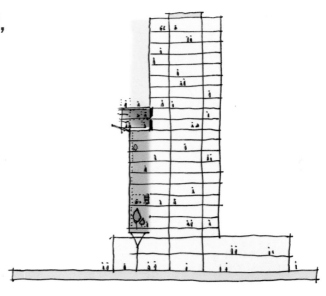

10

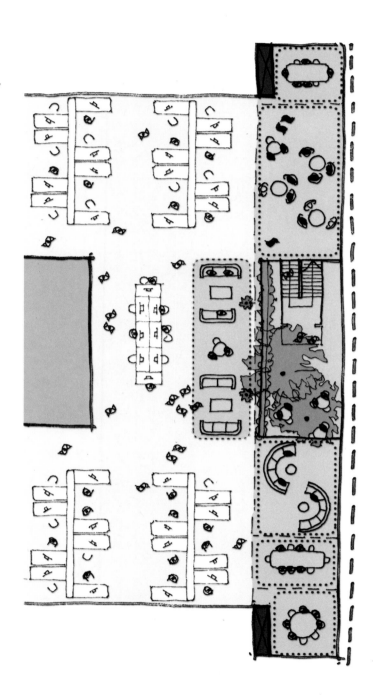

The second skin on the new external face allows a greater passive buffer zone for seasonal adjustments. Using trickle vents, planting for shade, internal partitions on the old façade line can be closed to insulate or retain heat during periods of excessive cool/hot. Vitiated air may be drawn through a "double-skin façade". Light shelves and louvres are incorporated to reduce direct or excessive solar gain, whilst reflecting light further into the floor-plate.

High rise buildings have been traditionally set back from the street frontage with the incorporation of a podium. This zone which was designed to set buildings away from streets may be partially or wholly sacrificed to allow buildings to have a true second life. It might be that by populating this zone, the street linings themselves become more active and greener.

The dead load of the new structure will most likely need to be taken vertically through the podium base, although floor extensions could also be 'hung' depending on the depth of the north face zone and the strength of the structural frame. Concrete framed buildings, having cured over time, will have substantial additional strength and stiffness, meaning that lateral and vertical loads could be supported without additional strengthening.

Furthermore construction might well be possible on a floor-by-floor basis, using the existing façade as the construction hoarding barrier and then breaking through for occupation. Thus the phasing allows continuous occupation.

Architecturally, it is clear that every building will have different issues and requirements, and maybe this solution cannot be employed into the historically important one-off, unique or special forms; however, many bland structures may well be substantially improved and humanised by 'adjuncts' that hang from some or all of their floors, adding vibrancy and life to their periphery that is currently absent. **Ⓑ**

COMPLETED FAÇADE OF THE ST BOTOLPH BUILDING

The St Botolph Building, a new commercial project in the City of London, provides an opportunity to streamline circulation systems by using innovative twin lift technology.

The St Botolph Building
London, United Kingdom

CIRCULATION STRATEGIES

Ewan Jones
Partner

The St Botolph Building in London, a landmark development by Minerva plc, is Grimshaw's largest commercial office scheme to date. Providing over 52,000 sq m (560,000 sq ft) of lettable space, it is located on an 'island' site near Aldgate, within the City, London's oldest and most prestigious commercial business district. The building has been designed for multiple tenancies, with nearly half the space already let to two occupiers: insurance brokers Lockton and law firm Clyde and Co.

Grimshaw began designing a building for the site in 1997 and the current scheme, now in the final stages of construction, was developed from a planning consent gained in 1999. In the spring of 2006, Minerva asked Grimshaw to update the 1999 plans and ensure that construction could begin within 12 months.

With nearly 10 years of change in the London office market since the project began, we took the opportunity to review the internal planning. The design strategy for the building proved to be robust, and remains unchanged; however internally the detailed execution incorporates major developments.

To provide maximum occupational flexibility, Grimshaw's design places the circulation and service cores at the outer edges of the floor plate. This balanced layout of four perimeter cores creates space suitable for the broadest possible range of occupiers including small-scale dealer operations.

With the two lowest office levels identified as potential dealing floors, the passenger lifts (elevators) could not be located centrally as this would interrupt the open plan space required for trading. In the 1999 scheme, the lifts were grouped in one enlarged perimeter core whilst two atria brought daylight into the centre of the building but stopped above the dealer floors.

Although the building has only 13 office floors, the floor plates are larger than commonly found in central London commercial buildings; up to 3,900 sq m (42,000 sq ft) of lettable area each.

01

02

01 COMPUTER GENERATED AERIAL VIEW OF THE PROJECT'S LOCATION AT THE EASTERN EDGE OF THE CITY OF LONDON

02 EARLY IMAGE OF MAIN ENTRANCE ON HOUNDSDITCH PRODUCED FOR MARKETING TO POTENTIAL TENANTS

To adequately service these floors, lift capacity analysis suggested a system that one might expect in a much higher building; 14 lifts split into a group of eight serving the lower floors and a further group of six serving the upper floors.

These two lift groups dominated one end of the floor plate, even if one group was placed in a central atrium, and did not provide ideal access to any floors that would potentially need to be divided into smaller sub-tenancies. Working closely with specialist consultants Preston Dynamics, the vertical circulation strategy became subject to intense scrutiny.

The design team also started to explore more innovative lifting technology. Double deck lifts (two passenger cabins fixed one above the other and moving together) would have reduced the number

of lift shafts and freed up valuable floor space, but they also come with some significant disadvantages. For example, users experience "false stops" as passengers in the linked cabin get in or out. Also, the lift cars are much heavier, requiring bigger motors and heavy duty running gear. In the St Botolph Building we also had different floor to floor heights to cope with. This would have required the double deck lift cars to be 'articulated' with the two cabins moving closer together or further apart. Again, this meant more weight and more money, along with the higher risk of breakdown. Ultimately, the high cost and poorer service killed this option.

In the interim, between gaining planning permission in 1999 and the project re-commencement in 2006, lift technology had also improved markedly.

To gain maximum efficiency in large lift installations, manufacturers had developed computerised systems that respond to user demand. Typically referred to now as "Destination Selection Control" (DSC), users first select a destination floor and are then directed to use a specific lift car instead of taking the first lift moving in the appropriate direction and then choosing their destination floor when inside the lift car.

This technology allows all journeys within the lift group to be co-ordinated by allocating the most appropriate car for each user's journey. Ten years ago when the St Botolph Building was first designed, this was new technology, and treated with some scepticism by developers and their tenants. By 2006, assisted by widespread use in new towers across the globe, DSC was readily accepted by London tenants and the letting agents whose advice oils the office development machine. This acceptance was a crucial tipping point for real innovation in lift technology.

As a next step in the evolution of lifts, the idea of running two lift cars independently in the one lift shaft was explored. Once DSC was accepted, it became a real possibility. The DSC system allows the movement of two lift cars to be safely and efficiently co-ordinated. This emerging technology provided a better answer for the St Botolph Building, and the opportunity to do something innovative. In the autumn of 2006 the project team began to investigate dual lifts in detail.

The substantial benefits of the system were immediately obvious. Instead of 14 shafts we needed only 8, with smaller lift cars (21 person instead 26 or 24 person). Not only did this increase the lettable office area, it allowed all the passenger lifts to be located within a single group housed in a dramatic 13-storey central atrium. This in turn allowed the combined lift core and atrium to continue down through one end of the dealer floors, linking directly to the reception space, whilst above the atrium could take a stepped form to become three times larger at its highest point. Combined with the perimeter core strategy, the addition of bridges in the atrium could provide direct access to four separate sub-tenancies on each floor, with no additional lobbies or corridors in the office space. .

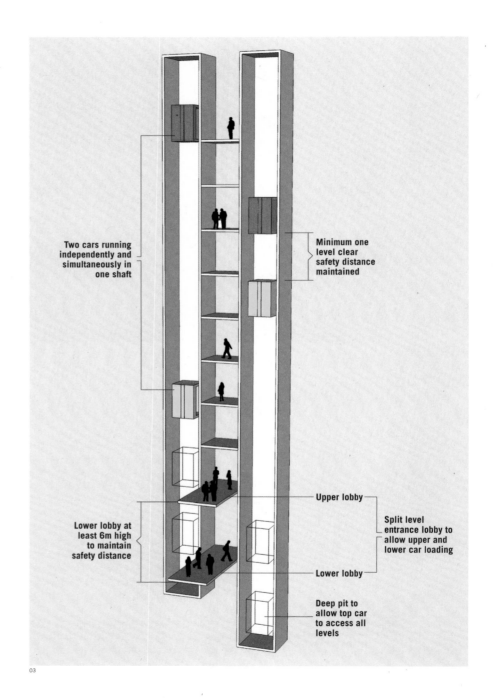

Two cars running independently and simultaneously in one shaft

Minimum one level clear safety distance maintained

Lower lobby at least 6m high to maintain safety distance

Upper lobby

Split level entrance lobby to allow upper and lower car loading

Lower lobby

Deep pit to allow top car to access all levels

03

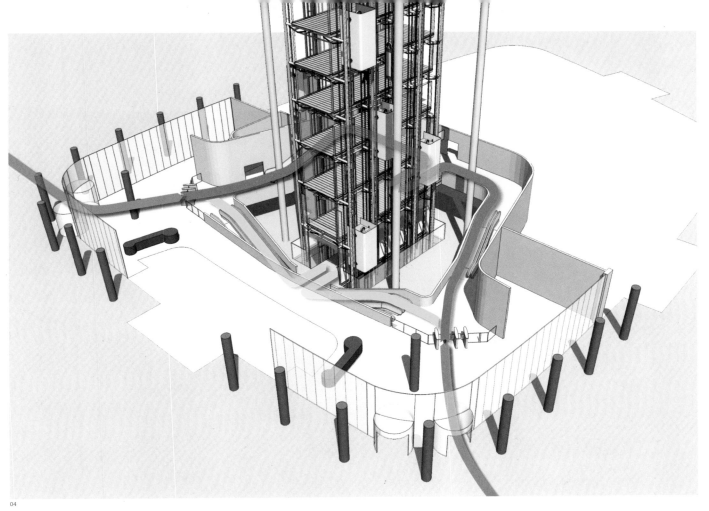

04

03 OPERATIONAL DIAGRAM FOR
    TWIN LIFT SYSTEM
04 DESIGN DEVELOPMENT OF
    GROUND FLOOR RECEPTION
    HALL. ESCALATORS PROVIDE
    ACCESS FROM GROUND LEVEL
    TO THE UPPER (RED) AND
    LOWER (YELLOW) LIFT LOBBIES

The lift car structures, running gear and motors are the same as conventional lifts, although the lift motor room is rather more congested. Maintenance costs were predicted to be 12% lower than conventional lifts as there would be fewer shafts and landing doors. The 2.2% premium on capital cost was more than offset by the 16,000 sq ft increase in lettable area.

This combination of space planning, technical, and architectural design advantages provided a compelling design case for this lifting strategy but there were other issues to be resolved.

Only one company, Thyssen Krupp, has developed the knowledge and equipment to manufacture what they call the "TWIN" lift system. Thyssen's TWIN system employs a four level safety concept ensuring that the cars maintain a minimum clear distance from each other during operation. This includes two entirely separate computer location systems for the lift cars, either of which can shut the system down.

In 2006, Thyssen had a working system that had been installed on a small scale within a few buildings in Germany, including one example in their own head office, and a large order for a scheme in Moscow. The TWIN system was not certified for use in the UK, although an application had been made and approval was anticipated by the end of 2006.

If we were to go ahead, this would be TWIN's first use in a UK office development, indeed their first use in new build in the UK and the biggest TWIN installation ever commissioned. To add to the ambition, we wanted to locate the lifts in an atrium so they would also be TWIN scenic lift shafts.

The office development world (or perhaps more precisely some tenants and their advisors) can be quite conservative and wary of anything that might be judged risky or 'different'. With the advantages of TWIN lifts established, Minerva and the design team began a careful evaluation process. This included discussion with letting agents, technical reviews, inspection of existing installations and a host of detailed due diligence work. At the conclusion of this process, the biggest concern was the risk inherent in a commitment to one supplier at an early stage in the design and procurement process. If the full design advantages of TWIN lifts were to be taken, the design could not easily be changed back at a later stage.

In January 2007 Minerva committed to use TWIN lifts for the St Botolph Building. Thyssen Krupp was appointed to help the design team prepare contract information, and our detailed design work began.

Adoption of the TWIN lift strategy had a huge impact on the building design, especially at the building entrance. To work efficiently, TWIN lifts need two loading levels at the ground floor, so that

both cars can be fully utilised for peak traffic flows. This immediately led to a concern about one level, and hence some users, being seen as 'second class', especially if this involved moving down from the entrance doors in order to go up in the building.

To serve well over 5,000 occupants, the reception design that Grimshaw developed occupies half of the building at ground level. Much of this space is carved away in the centre of the entrance hall where the lifts are located, so that the ground floor becomes a large 6m high balcony surrounding a 10m high central arena that opens into the stepped atrium above.

The upper lift cars are accessed from a glass bridge mezzanine within reception whilst the lower lift lobby is part of the generous lower ground level which benefits from the building's social facilities that will be grouped here when fit-out is completed. The client's ambition in this space is to create the same sense of service and comfort provided in Virgin Airline's upper class lounges. Both levels are accessed by paired escalators, running alongside bespoke aluminium 'blade' clad walls that guide

05 **DESIGN DEVELOPMENT PROGRESS DURING 2006 (FROM LEFT TO RIGHT) ILLUSTRATING FLOOR SPACE GAINED WITH TWIN LIFTS**

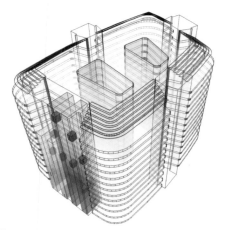 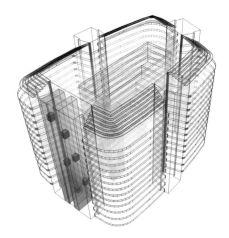 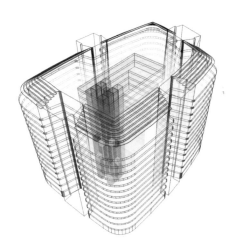

05

06

08

08

**06 COMPLETED UPPER LOBBY
LEVEL WITH DSC SCREENS AND
ALUMINIUM 'BLADE' WALL**
**07 DSC SCREEN DESIGN WITH
BESPOKE GRAPHICS FOR
TOUCHSCREEN INTERFACE**

**08 COMPLETED LIFT INSTALLATION
WITH RED (UPPER) CARS
WAITING AT HIGH LEVEL AND
YELLOW (LOWER) LIFT CAR IN
OPERATION**

07

users through the space.

The reception hall provides the first view of the lift core that is the centrepiece of the building's interior design. This 16-storey steel structure places a kinetic sculpture in the central atrium, with movement of the 16 lift cars and their counterweights visible throughout the heart of the building. We deliberately set out to celebrate and display the engineering of the structure and the systems: all of the steelwork and lift gear is exposed against the calmer background of the surrounding atrium wall cladding. The walls, floors and soffits of the lift lobbies are all glass and where bridges to the office floors are required, they are supported off the lift core's steelwork with a "drawbridge" design that clearly shows how the loads are taken back into the main structure.

09

09 COMPUTER GENERATED VIEW OF
RECEPTION HALL AT ENTRANCE
FROM HOUNDSDITCH

We felt that glazed lift cars might be a step too far for user comfort and with the lively activity of people and carefully crafted engineering components surrounding them, it was decided that the lift car interiors should provide a moment of calm. The interiors maximise contrast with their immediate surroundings and continue the white marble floor of the reception area allied to other simple high quality finishes, including stainless steel and glossy white walls and ceilings.

During our visits to the Thyssen Krupp factory we had been intrigued by their colour coding of all the TWIN lift gear. This is used for safety, helping maintenance staff to identify which set of equipment they are working on although in the only scenic installation that we had seen, the colour coding had been minimised in the public zones.

Continuing our aim of exploiting and celebrating the engineering design we spotted the potential for colour coding to provide another layer of interest. With blue as the building's main exterior colour, led by the blue glass spandrel panel in the external walls, we selected the remaining two primary colours for the passenger lift system.

For these key elements we sought more subtlety than simple boxes of colour. The outer three walls facing the office floors are silver aluminium planes that extend beyond the roof car and floor to engage with and shield the lift slings and running gear. Cool and calm, smooth and business-like, they continue the theme of curved corners and overlapping planes used in the blue glass exterior walls of the building. However, like a bright lining to a sober business suit, the aluminium skin shields a burst

of colour. The lid, underside and doors of the lifts are bright red (upper cars) or acid yellow (lower cars) and can clearly be seen from the glazed lift lobby as the lift arrives and even glimpsed from the office space through the lobby's glass walls. The exceptionally tall thin counterweights then use a reversed layout with coloured frames surrounding a silver skin.

Attention to detail in engineering and construction is a fundamental part of Grimshaw's design philosophy. The St Botolph Building is at the upper end of the office building spectrum in the UK, seeking high rents even in the depths of recession. Therefore everything in this project, to continue the tailoring metaphor, is bespoke. Indicator panels in the lift cars, lift guide rail support brackets and lift shaft signage all use themes that are developed

10

10 BRIDGES ACROSS THE ATRIUM
    ALLOW SEVERAL FLOORS TO
    HAVE INDIVIDUAL ACCESS FOR
    MULTIPLE TENANTS

11 TWO LOWER LIFT CARS IN A
    TYPICAL LOBBY WITH GLASS
    FLOORS AND WALLS AND A DSC
    LIFT CALL SCREEN

11

throughout the building's components to provide a consistent and common design language.

Within the TWIN lift system, implementing the client's and architect's design ambition has been hugely helped by Thyssen Krupp's engineering resources and heritage. Unusually for a lift company, they manufacture almost all of their own components, from electronic circuit boards to motor pulleys. When we needed a stainless steel skirting in the lift cars that was folded and curved without welding, the skills to make it were found in Thyssen's team that make the casings for escalators.

The obsession with detail and quality has extended to the smallest parts, including the LCD touch screens where users interact with the DSC system. User expectations for electronic systems have been hugely raised over recent years by well-designed consumer products like the iPhone and it is easy for components in buildings to look very clunky and dated in comparison. Here Grimshaw saw an opportunity to develop and improve the standard product. With no new operating components, but intelligent reorganisation, packaging and graphics, we undertook significant product development. This included turning the LCD screen through 90 degrees, a new stainless steel housing, bespoke graphics by Grimshaw and concealed swipe card readers.

Writing in May 2010, this ambitious scheme is about to be realised. The final stages of production are underway, installation on site is nearly complete and commissioning has begun for the first tenants to take occupation in June. The project team has risen to the challenges and our client has been rewarded for their brave decision with a unique building that has wowed visitors already. By September, all works will be complete and the St Botolph Building will host a party to celebrate 30 years since the Grimshaw practice was founded. **B**

With thanks to the teams at Minerva, Thyssen Krupp, Preston Dynamics, CMF and Skanska

SECTION TWO
STRUCTURES

SOUTHERN CROSS STATION DURING CONSTRUCTION

During the design development phase of the Pulkovo Airport project, the use of innovative modelling techniques allowed the rapid comparison and assessment of numerous options.

Pulkovo Airport
St Petersburg, Russian Federation

SURFACES AS STRUCTURE

Chris Crombie
Associate

With additional material by
Mark Middleton and **Eduard Ross**

When we started to design the competition for the new international terminal in St Petersburg we asked ourselves 'why is it that when you arrive at most airports around the globe you feel like you could be anywhere in the world?'

We wanted things to be different with our design for St Petersburg. We wanted to represent the uniqueness of the city; its setting by the river Neva, the rich cultural heritage and its Arctic climate in our designs. Arrival at Pulkovo should feel like arriving in the city. In order to do this without resorting to pastiche or compromising the functional and operational requirements of a modern airport, we started to look at the city's climate and how a response to the environment could influence our design.

St Petersburg is the world's most northern city of over 1 million inhabitants. Located at 59 degrees 57' North, it shares its latitude with Oslo in Norway, the southern tip of Greenland and Seward in Alaska.

Climatically the city is influenced by both the cold continental tundra of Russia to the East and moderated by the Baltic Sea to the west. The confluence of these two forces creates a humid continental climate of short, warm, humid summers but long, hard cold winters.

On average the city is covered by snow for over 120 days per year with temperatures dropping to as low as -35DegC (-33DegF) in January. During the winter months there is less than six hours of sunlight per day with the angle of the sun not rising above 10 degrees. Conversely, between the months of May and July, the city remains bright for almost 19 hours per day with the remaining hours stalled in a perpetual dusk. These months are known locally as the 'white nights'.

Local people have learnt to live with this uncompromising climate and have adapted their buildings to make the best of their climate. Their designs are notable by their need to catch and control daylight, deal with snow (when frozen and melting) and provide protection from the extremes of temperature.

01 ST PETERSBURG'S URBAN FABRIC IS CHARACTERISED BY A SERIES OF INTERCONNECTING ISLANDS, CANALS AND BRIDGES

02 A CLIMATE DOMINATED BY LONG COLD WINTERS, HEAVY SNOWFALLS AND BELOW ZERO TEMPERATURES

CLIMATICALLY THE CITY IS INFLUENCED BY BOTH THE CONTINENTAL TUNDRA OF RUSSIA AND THE MODERATING INFLUENCE OF THE BALTIC SEA.

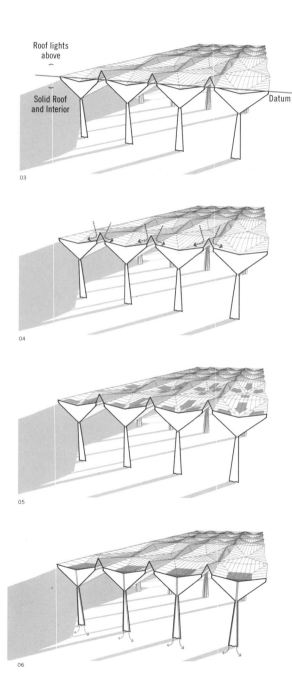

Roof lights above

Solid Roof and Interior

Datum

03

04

05

06

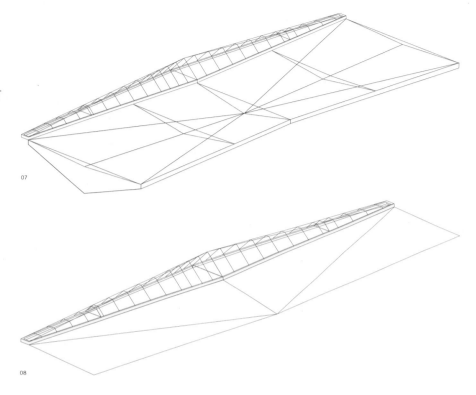

07

08

03 THE EXTERNAL ROOF SURFACE IS DEFINED BY A HORIZONTAL DATUM CONDITION
04 SNOW IS ABLE TO SETTLE BELOW THIS LINE WITH THE GLASS ROOF LIGHTS PROJECTING ABOVE
05 THE ROOF'S FLAT 'HOPPERS' CHANNEL THE MELTING / DRIFTING SNOW TO THE POINTS OF GREATEST STRUCTURAL SUPPORT
06 MELT WATER IS COLLECTED IN THE CENTRAL PORTION OF THE ROOF 'HOPPER' AND INTEGRATED BACK INTO THE TERMINAL'S DRAINAGE SYSTEM
07 THE ROOF HOPPERS ARE FORMED BY A SERIES OF FOLDED, TRIANGULAR PLANES
08 GLASS ROOF LIGHTS PROJECT ABOVE THE ROOF LINE, MAXIMISING FUNCTIONALITY OVER THE COURSE OF THE YEAR

This has structured, shaped and coloured the appearance of the city and largely defined its architectural character. It is this character, along with its climate, that has provided the main influence for our design of the new International Terminal 2 at Pulkovo Airport in St Petersburg.

For airport terminals, due to their very size, the roof is the most dominant and recognisable element. In the simplest sense, it is required to protect those beneath from the extremes of the external environment and in St Petersburg this relates mainly to snow.

Any snowfall in St Petersburg can sit for prolonged periods, sometimes for months and at depths of over 2m thick. Our main consideration was to design the roof to avoid snow drifting,

09

which can result in uneven loading of the structure. In response to this, the roof is predominantly flat with minimal relief over its surface ensuring that snow accumulates as evenly as possible across its 50,000 sq m surface.

Where snow falls it eventually melts, so our roof design also had to deal with lots of meltwater and the period in spring when the diurnal range in temperatures can be between +/- 10 Deg C. This means that the snow melts during the day but refreezes at night. To deal with this the falls in the flat roof are arranged as subtle, inverted prisms resembling flat hoppers with their lowest points directly above the centreline of each column. This allows the deepest build-up of snow to be above the point of greatest structural support and meltwater to be collected at the natural point for drainage.

After snow, the second environmental consideration for the roof design was how we used natural daylight within the building. Roof lights were the natural starting point for us to get daylight deep into the heart of the building. In order that they may remain effective throughout the year, particularly during winter when sunlight is at a premium, the prism-like roof lights, reminiscent of crystals of ice, project above the flat roof datum to a height of over 4 metres at the centre then tapering away sharply along the length of a roof module. This ensures that even when snow lies thick on the roof the roof lights will still retain their effectiveness.

The influences of the local climate have therefore had a great effect on us whilst developing the aesthetic of the roof as a whole.

Internally the soffit is arranged as a series of flat triangular panels apparently folded around the structure of the roof. The resultant geometrical appearance, reminiscent of ice fractals, defines the character of the airport's internal spaces. The soffit rises between the columns to add volume and space beneath and is then carved to enforce the intuitive direction passengers travel to get to the planes. This movement is reinforced by the natural light from the roof lights running in the same direction.

To maximise the effect of the roof lights, a reflector is positioned within its structure to reduce glare by redirecting the rays of the low angle winter sun. It is also designed to gild and soften the light

which it reflects through the use of gold-coloured materials, creating a golden hue to the surface of the soffit which receives the light.

Gilding light in this way is an effect characterised by the incidental reflections from the gilded domes and spires of St Petersburg's most prominent buildings and brings a signature from the historic city into the heart of the new terminal.

The roof and soffit treatment have emerged from the design process to become the defining identity of Pulkovo's redevelopment. From concept to detail it has been subject to careful consideration and investigation. This has been undertaken through the use of some computer models but more usefully for the client and ourselves has been the development of physical models of increasing size and complexity.

At the beginning, the concept of a folded surface was clear in our collective consciousness and was initially investigated with the use of traditional origami and paper-folding methods and techniques. Creased paper and card maquettes were created to explore and investigate the subtleties of the

geometry and the need for the surface to alter in height and depth. These models allowed for quick and efficient evaluation of many diagrammatic approaches as well as the articulation of volume and linear space.

In addition to the physical realism of the models, these early explorations confirmed a clear relationship between the plan and a necessity for it to be permeated with light. This was investigated by introducing cuts into the folded surface to represent roof lights.

As we progressed with our ideas, the increasingly refined geometry demanded a more flexible form of representation. This resulted in our discovering an origami computer programme that was designed for children called Pepakura, originally conceived as a way to turn cartoon characters into folded paper models. We trialled it as a model-making tool and folding pattern generator. The software proved to be very useful allowing complex three dimensional computer drawings to be converted into simplistic two dimensional origami patterns. These could then be folded and assembled as paper models of our roof.

13

14

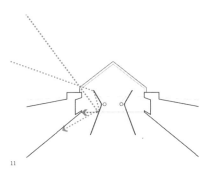

11

12

09 PASSENGER VIEW WITHIN
THE DEPARTURES CONCOURSE.
THE TRIANGULATED, GOLD
SURFACE FOLDS IN RESPONSE TO
STRUCTURE AND DAYLIGHT TO
FORM THE TERMINAL'S PRINCIPLE
ARCHITECTURAL FEATURE.
THE ROOF AREA IS FORMED BY
12 REPEATED ROOF 'STRIPS'.
EACH ROOF STRIP CONSISTS
OF 6 CONNECTED SHALLOW
HOPPERS OF VARYING LENGTHS.
EACH 'HOPPER' CORRESPONDS
WITH THE MAIN STRUCTURAL
ROOF SUPPORTS BELOW

11 LOW ANGLED SUNLIGHT IS
REDIRECTED AND GILDED ONTO
THE INTERNAL FOLDED SOFFIT

12 THE GILDED DOMES OF ST.
PETERSBURG'S CIVIC
ARCHITECTURE

13 EARLY EXPLORATION MODELS
INVESTIGATED THE NOTION
OF A CONTINUOUS SURFACE
ALTERING IN HEIGHT AND DEPTH
TO CREATE ENCLOSURE TO THE
MAIN INTERNAL SPACES

14 SLICING AND CUTTING WAS
EXPLORED AS A MEANS OF
INTRODUCING DAYLIGHT THROUGH
THE ORIGAMI SURFACES

This means of development allowed a rapid exploration of the folded surface but within the accuracy of CAD design development. It also bridged that gap between a cyber representation and the object itself. We found our ideas had greater meaning if they escaped the confines of the computer screen and were able to be held in the palm of our hands.

Key areas of evaluation included different surface reliefs, structural depths and location of principle soffit crease lines. Crucially this process allowed for many ideas to be tested efficiently in a short space of time, and to a high degree of realism. It also enabled a thorough exploration of options and a rounded evaluation of what could be achieved within the concept of a folded surface. Almost 100 maquettes were made using this process.

The next step beyond the 'Pepakura' process was to larger scale laser cut models which were procured to explore the spatial qualities of the soffit geometry in greater detail. These offered a similar speed of assembly to that of the card maquettes but with a higher degree of spatial simulation and

15

16

15 **LASER CUT MODELS WERE ASSEMBLED IN CONJUNCTION WITH COLUMN SUPPORTS TO EXPLORE THE SPATIAL QUALITY AND KEY HEIGHTS OF THE PRINCIPLE TERMINAL SPACES**

16 **ANALYSIS OF THE ROOF LIGHT DEFLECTORS AND QUALITY OF GILDED, GOLD REFLECTIONS**

THE MODEL DEMONSTRATED THE QUALITY OF LIGHT WHICH WOULD BE ACHIEVED WITHIN THE AREAS OF SOFFIT AROUND THE SKY-LIGHTS

on a much larger scale. Various combinations of the roof were built, from a single bay to three full strips, using timber veneers, metals and sprayed plastics.

This variety of model sizes offered us a detailed understanding of proportion and quality of space. The largest of these models was constructed at 1:75 scale. This was over 4.5m long and mounted at height so it can be viewed while standing beneath, offering a unique perspective of the idea. At this scale the model also demonstrated the quality of light which would be achieved within the areas of soffit around the roof lights, informing the design of the reflector in terms of materiality and reflective requirements.

Once we had the large scale models we could use them to explore the soffit details and their key inter-faces. The continual design development led to an emerging complexity of the folded surface but offered limited opportunity for interfacing elements such as columns or façade. Therefore modelling three dimensional junctions at up to 1:25 scale played an important role in understanding and resolving these detailed aspects of the design. One such area was the junction between column and soffit expressed as a column head. Modelled sections of roof and column explored the introduction of a continuous shadow gap detail between the roof plates which accommodated penetrations through the soffit.

The results of these investigations have led to a design that is unique to St Petersburg. The folded, angular roof soffit is distinctly of its time but it has been shaped by the timeless, influences of the local environment and the rich architectural heritage of the city. ⓑ

18

17 1:75 SCALE MODEL ASSEMBLED
    IN THE GRIMSHAW LONDON
    FRONT ATRIUM
18 EXTERNAL VIEW OF THE NEW
    TERMINAL FROM THE AIRPORT
    CITY DEVELOPMENT

19 LASER CUT MODEL AND
    FRAMEWORK TESTING SOFFIT
    FORM, ROOF LIGHT SIZINGS AND
    STRUCTURAL STRATEGIES

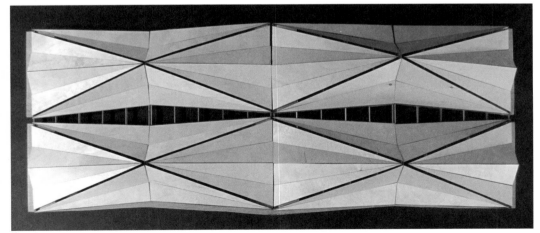

19

A good conceptual mo
predict the effects of o
good model we operat
do operations as we w
we can't fully appreciat
expect, or what to do if

del allows us to
ur actions. Without a
e by rote, blindly; we
ere told to do them;
e why, what effects to
things go wrong.

Donald A. Norman
The Design of Everyday Things

Using a geometry which is complex without being complicated, the design of the roof at the Horno³ Steel Museum serves both architectural and structural functions.

Horno³: Museo Del Acero
Monterrey, Mexico

FOLDED PLATE STRUCTURES

Christian Hönigschmid
Associate

Michael Blancato
Architect

Additional material by **Wilfried Laufs**
(for Werner Sobek)

Horno³: Museo Del Acero in Monterrey, Mexico, is comprised of two major elements: the restoration of a derelict 1960s blast furnace complex (recently designated as a National Industrial Heritage Site) and a new addition providing gallery space and other museum facilities.

The museum showcases the history of steel manufacturing, with exhibits as well as a pyrotechnical show; it also chronicles the industrial history of the state of Nuevo Leon and its capital Monterrey, which for much of the 20th Century was renowned for its steel production.

The architectural challenge was to balance sensitive historic preservation against the requirement for a new purpose for the complex as a dynamic symbol within its changed context – the surrounding steelworks having been converted into a public park. The building was completed in September 2007 when the city hosted the Universal Forum of Cultures.

The restored blast furnace complex comprises of an 80m high Blast Furnace, a 'Cast Hall' and an array of supporting facilities. Adjacent to the Furnace, located on the site of a former slag-heap, the new addition houses an entry wing, the main public stairs and an interactive gallery space: the Steel Gallery, which acts as an architectural focal point and a complementary component to the existing industrial elements. In order to work discreetly within the context of the blast furnace, this new gallery is largely subterranean, situated underneath a green roof that gently slopes down to the surrounding public park.

Both the refurbishment and new additions, interventions, etc. respond strongly to the site's history as a steelworks. This is made most explicit through a series of structural elements, including a single-span helical steel stair, a façade system and the folded – or more accurately, tessellated – Steel Gallery Roof.

01

THE ARCHITECTURAL CHALLENGE WAS TO BALANCE SENSITIVE HISTORIC PRESERVATION AGAINST THE REQUIREMENT FOR A NEW PROGRAM AND A DYNAMIC SYMBOL

01 DOMINATING ELEMENTS OF THE PROJECT ARE THE ACTUAL BLAST FURNACE INSIDE THE CENTER GIRDERWORK AND THE NEWLY-CLAD CAST HALL TO THE LEFT

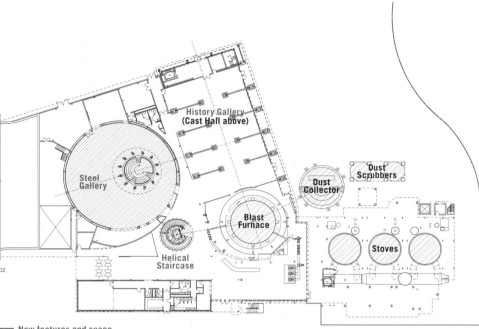

History Gallery
(Cast Hall above)

Steel
Gallery

Dust
Collector

Dust
Scrubbers

Blast
Furnace

Stoves

Helical
Staircase

02

— New features and space

— Existing features and space

02 THE BLAST FURNACE IS TREATED
AS A 'MIXING VALVE', THE
CENTRAL ORGANISING ELEMENT
FOR ALL EXISTING AND NEW
SPACES AND ELEMENTS
03 HOVERING OVER A GREEN ROOF
ON TOP OF THE STEEL GALLERY
ROOF, A TERRACE SERVES AS
A BREAK-OUT SPACE FOR THE
CAST HALL WHICH CAN BE
RENTED OUT FOR EVENTS

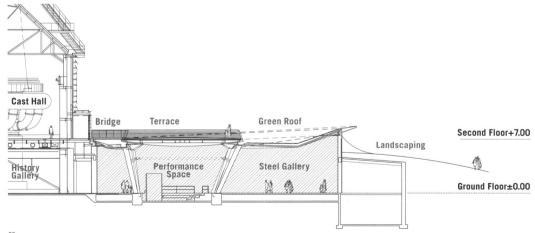

Cast Hall

Bridge   Terrace   Green Roof

Second Floor+7.00

Landscaping

History
Gallery

Performance
Space

Steel Gallery

Ground Floor±0.00

03

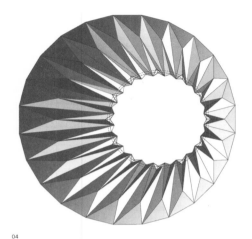

04

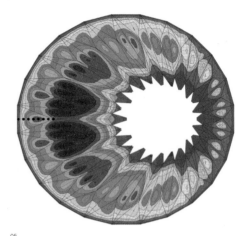

05

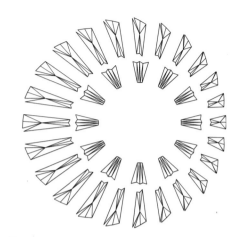

06

THE ROOF HAD TO CLEARLY EXPRESS THE STRUCTURAL FORCES PRESENT, AS WELL AS DEMONSTRATE THE ENGINEERING AND CONSTRUCTION POSSIBILITIES AFFORDED BY STEEL – TO SERVE AS AN EXHIBIT IN ITS OWN RIGHTS

For this important element we were striving to achieve the following ambitions:

● To ensure the roof functioned didactically, clearly expressing the structural forces present, as well as demonstrating the engineering and construction possibilities afforded by steel – serving as an exhibit in its own right.

● To achieve structural efficiency and utility, using material strength, structural design approach, connection and building-technology.

● To utilise geometry that simultaneously responded to planning constraints and incorporated other important considerations such as rainwater collection.

● To function architecturally for both spaces, above and below – the former manifested as a planted roof landscape open to the surrounding park, and as the ceiling and container of the Steel Gallery below.

With those goals in mind, it became clear early on that we wanted to demonstrate the structural possibilities and capabilities of steel in a unique and rather unusual way, from an architectural but even more so an engineering point of view. Rather than the common post and beam/truss system where the steel members are all linear elements, we sought to use steel plates, to create a structurally performative surface. All those plates are planar triangles; this means no bending or complicated distortion was necessary. This initiative corresponded flawlessly with the idea of introducing folds into the surface to create the demand for rigidity that a structure of this scale requires, but without adding any further mass. We merged the commonly separated skin and bones of a building into a single form.

A space resembling a geode served as a further

04 EARLY ROOF DIAGRAM DURING SCHEMATIC DESIGN, CAPTURING THE CORE IDEA OF FOLDED SURFACE COMPRISED ONLY OF PLANAR TRIANGLES. MISSING IS STILL ONE FURTHER ADDITIONAL FOLD IN THE PERIMETER TRIANGLE WHICH WAS STRUCTURALLY REQUIRED TO DEAL WITH LOCAL PLATE-BUCKLING

05 COMPUTED STRESS ANALYSIS, EMPLOYING A 3-D FINITE ELEMENT MODEL THE ROOF, COLUMNS AND TERRACE CANTILEVERS. THE DOTTED LINE INDICATES THE ADDITIONAL FOLD

06 UNFOLDED SEGMENTS OF ROOF AND COLUMNS. THE FOLDED ROOF SEGMENTS CAN BE THEORETICALLY CREATED FROM A SINGLE FLAT SHEET WITH ONLY ONE CUT-OUT REQUIRED

07 PARAMETRIC MODEL DIAGRAM A: ALL NODE POINTS OF THE FOLDS ARE LOCATED ON A SERIES OF NON-CONCENTRIC CIRCLES

08 PARAMETRIC MODEL DIAGRAM B: BASED ON STRUCTURAL NEEDS FOR DEPTHS OF THE SPANNING SEGMENTS EACH NODE POINT RECEIVED A DISCRETE Z-VALUE AS AN OFF-SET

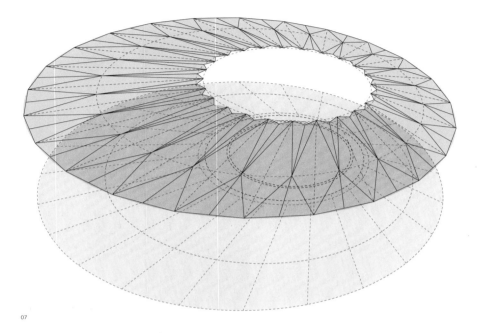

07

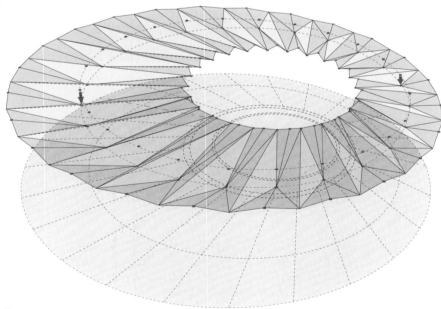

08

analogy; a geometrically precise, yet hidden interior, formed as a result of imposed external forces, with a rough and more naturalistic exterior. As this building merges with the landscape, we perceive a hidden, subterranean jewel-like space nestled within the natural surroundings of the green roof and adjacent to a raw steel wall which serves to delineate it from the other museum zones. This space is meant to be discovered and revealed to visitors as they journey through the museum.

On a project-wide scale a more formal relationship exists between the circular nature of the existing supporting facilities arrayed around the blast furnace and the newly constructed helical stair and rounded Steel Gallery, placed to draw from and reinforce this organisation. Functionally, the circular space works well with the exhibit design's programmatic necessity of a central performance space comprising a stage and tiered seating. Mainly interactive exhibits are arranged radially around this performance space, along the visitor's path of circulation. To create a more dynamic space and satisfy differing exhibition requirements, the performance space was designed and located asymmetrically.

With the planning, basic-form, and structural concept in place, we started to develop the specific geometry of the roof. With the help of a parametric computer model, a set of geometric relationships was established, allowing adaptive structural shaping and responsiveness to further constraints as the design evolved.

Examples of these additional functional and spatial constraints are the minimum slopes to assure effective drainage and clearance below the bridge, which connects the terrace with the Cast Hall.

In order to achieve a load-bearing and self-supporting structure, with the largest span of 13m (43ft) and a diameter of 30m (98ft), the design relied on extensively calculated stress analyses which allowed the optimisation of the design and the advance of the known engineering limits of structural steel. With the use of a 3D finite element model, deformations and stress peaks were evaluated as well as plate buckling limits taken into consideration; these limits were found; these limits ultimately proved to be the main structural driver for the roof design.

To address local buckling and varying spans as well as to minimise stresses, the structural heights and plate thicknesses were adjusted iteratively. With a maximum fold-depth of 1.5m (~5ft) the steel plates could be kept relatively thin, thicknesses vary between 10 and 20mm; column plates have a thickness of 13mm. Additional folds were added to the geometry where increased plate thickness alone would not suffice; further beams or stiffeners were not required throughout the entire structure. As the spans increase, the depth of the folds also gradually increase; this is clearly visible from underneath.

Within the central ring of columns and the series of radiating roof segments, there exist compressive forces which push to the perimeter. These forces are offset by a closed tension ring system which works due to the roof's circular nature, i.e. the structure is in equilibrium.

Additional elements were designed independently of the parametric model, but their implications were recorded in it. The 12 main structural support columns for example, were initially considered

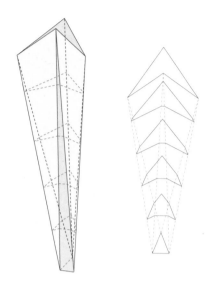

07

THE DESIGN REQUIRED CLOSE CO-ORDINATION FROM THE OUTSET BETWEEN THE STRUCTURAL ENGINEERS, THE FABRICATOR AND GRIMSHAW

a Outer setout circle r=15.15m
b Inner setout circle r= 5.0m
c Faceted columns (12), base section: triangular, top section: chevron (t=13mm)
d Edge beams faceted in plan, double-tapering in section
e Transfer ring beam (behind wall cladding)
f Perimeter support column (behind wall cladding)
g Triangulated roof plates (24 sections), varying thickness according to requirements (t= 10-20mm)
h Faceted collar to support glass block ring (t=10mm)
i Cantilevering terrace supports (12), tapering chevron section (t = 13mm)
j Terrace support structure, RHS and fabricated curved sections

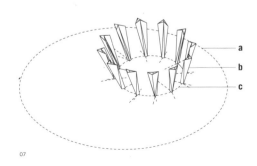

07

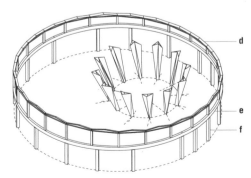

as single plates with one fold, but to provide the required structural rigidity and movement connections at the top, a multi-faceted and hollow profile that transitions or 'lofts' from a chevron to a triangle was developed. This allows for column-integrated roof drainage and sprinklers to keep the underside free of any surface-mounted infrastructure.

To incorporate architectural lighting as well as theatrical light fixtures for the stage, we designed a circular boom: a trough with a single fold, cantilevered inwards from the inner column ring.

In a similar fashion, tapering chevron-cantilevers reach out to support the terrace which hovers over the folded roof, separated by a ring of glass-blocks to distinguish the two elements architecturally. The terrace structure, sitting with omni-directional sliding joints on those cantilevers, is laterally restrained through the bridge to the main building.

Along with the usual set of drawings, the steel fabricators received a simple 3D model of the finalised geometry containing only surfaces with zero thickness. To those surfaces they had to apply the required thickness, inwards in the case of the columns and upwards at the roof segments to maintain the architectural intent.

During collaborative workshops we also developed a clear methodology of prefabricating all 24 segments and 12 columns in the shop as well as

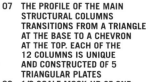

07 THE PROFILE OF THE MAIN STRUCTURAL COLUMNS TRANSITIONS FROM A TRIANGLE AT THE BASE TO A CHEVRON AT THE TOP. EACH OF THE 12 COLUMNS IS UNIQUE AND CONSTRUCTED OF 5 TRIANGULAR PLATES
08 1/3 SCALE MOCK-UP OF ONE OF THE SHORTER ROOF SEGMENTS IN THE FABRICATOR'S SHOP, WITH THE PLATE ASSEMBLY
09 DIFFERENT DEGREES OF SANDBLASTING FOR SURFACE TREATMENT WERE TESTED ON THE 1/3 SCALE MOCKUP TO DETERMINE FINAL ARCHITECTURAL FINISH
10 ONE OF THE SHOP-ASSEMBLED ROOF SEGMENTS IS CRANED IN
11 AXONOMETRIC BUILD-UP OF ALL COMPONENTS OF THE ROOF STRUCTURE

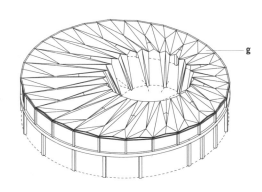
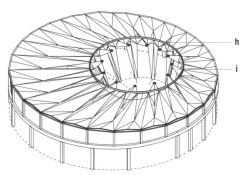
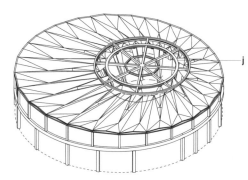

the assembly sequence on site.

This approach was validated by the construction of several essential models at full, ½ and ⅓ scale. Through this process the fabricator gained important experience in plate assembly and welding procedures which proved invaluable when it came to achieving consistent edges with sharp angles. Furthermore, the mock-ups served to test various means of on-site erection and the final surface finish.

As a further advantage to shop-fabrication all elements were inspected before being shipped to site as part of a stringent quality management regime. All these efforts ultimately enabled increased accuracy as well as the minimisation of on-site welding and the reduction of installation time. The final structure behaves like monolithic folded surface as its prefabricated segments are continuously and fully welded and the craned-in segments continuously bolted.

The landscaped berms, in addition to the roof around the Steel Gallery, are vegetated and predominantly planted with native Love Grass, which is a species adapted to the low rainfall typical of Northern Mexico. The Steel Gallery roof itself is planted with a quilt of flowering sedums that follow the form of the tessellated structure below. In all cases the vegetation has been specifically selected to reduce maintenance and irrigation, as well as being designed to provide habitats for local forms of wildlife and a resting spot for the annual butterfly migration that passes through the area.

This absolutely performance-based design demonstrates how, with today's computer-aided technology, steel as a sheet material is able to be transformed into structurally rigid forms by complex folding. From the outset, using this technique required close co-ordination and collaboration between the structural engineers (Werner Sobek), the Mexican fabricator (Paileria San Luis Potosi) and the Grimshaw team. We are delighted that the end result, as well as being a very rewarding iterative process, also, enabled the creation of a roof that serves manifold architectural and structural functions with the deployment of a highly specific geometry, which is complex without being complicated. ❷

08

09

10

11

12

13

08 ROOF DRAINAGE IS INTEGRATED AT EACH OF THE CONCRETE PEDESTALS FOR THE 12 INNER STRUCTURAL COLUMNS; THE RAINWATER IS COLLECTED IN A CISTERN AND REUSED FOR IRRIGATION

09 ACROSS EACH ROOF SEGMENT, THE TEMPORARY BRACINGS WERE USED TO CRANE IN THE SEGMENTS. THEY WERE REMOVED AFTERWARDS

10 ALL SEGMENTS ARE CONTINUOUSLY BOLTED TOGETHER TO ACHIEVE STRUCTURALLY THE MONOLITHIC FOLDED SURFACE. ALSO IN PLACE IS THE STEEL FRAMING FOR BRIDGE AND TERRACE, WHICH SITS ON ITS SUPPORTS WITH A SLIDING CONNECTION

11 DIFFERENT TYPES OF DRAUGHT-TOLERANT AND FLOWERING SEDUMS MAP THE GEOMETRY OF THE STEEL STRUCTURE BELOW. THOSE SEDUMS REQUIRE VERY LITTLE IRRIGATION AND ONLY MINIMAL MAINTENANCE. THE TERRACE OFFERS VIEWS OVER PARQUE FUNDIDORA AND A GREAT DOMINATING MOUNTAIN RANGE TO THE SOUTH OF THE CITY

12 WITH ALL ROOF SEGMENTS IN PLACE, LIGHT IS STILL POURING INTO THE SPACE THROUGH THE CENTRAL OPENING BEFORE THE CONSTRUCTION OF THE TERRACE SLAB

13 INTERACTIVE EXHIBITS (DESIGNED BY ALDRICHPEARS ASSOCIATES) RADIATE AROUND THE INNER RING OF COLUMNS WHICH ENCLOSES THE PERFORMANCE SPACE

Nature teaches us that ecosystems ar made up of habitat — local experts

e
specialists
who know how to
work the system

Janine M. Benyus
Biomimicry: Innovation Inspired by Nature

Double-curved cable-net structures using three dimensions to create light, efficient and beautiful design solutions.

Fulton Street Transit Center
New York, USA

Coney Island Center
New York, USA

DOING MORE WITH LESS

Paulo Faria
Associate

Michael Stein
Schlaich, Bergermann and Partners

Before exploring the recent work Grimshaw has been undertaking using cable-net structures, it may be opportune to define the subject matter a little.

Cables and their most common companions, fabrics, are traditional building materials that can be traced back historically to the origin of human settlements and the move from nomadism to more sedentary agricultural societies. Initially, what we now call cables were used primarily for ensuring the stability of built structures, to resist wind and to stabilise fabric enclosures supported by masts.

The modern fully locked steel cable is the result of centuries of design evolution and can trace its ancestry back to the braided organic fibres that were used in pre-historic times. Naturally occurring lengths of plant fibre were the first 'cables' and their use in hunting, towing, fastening, attaching, and carrying, was the result of the inherent benefit of its tensile strength.

The use of cables becomes preferable and indeed recommended when the design brief requires the creation of light structures that are able to capitalise on the advantages made available by use of the tensile strength. In order for this to occur, a specific shape needs to be established for the optimum performance of the structure. The term "formfinding" suggests the act of investigation and examination that eventually leads to the final form being determined. This search for the "form" may seem to be quite arbitrary; why at a certain point is the shape of a structure 'found'? What are the parameters?

Initially there are the obvious architectural and functional ones, but there are also structural parameters that, especially with respect to lightweight structures, often govern the process of formfinding.

In the case of the simplest structural systems – the catenary cable, or curve, formed when the cable is subjected to uniform force (such as gravity) – the form depends on the loading assumptions and the maximum forces in the elements the designers are

01

NATURAL LIGHT WAS RECOGNISED AS AN IMPERITIVE COMPONENT OF THE DESIGN IN TERMS OF SERVING TO CLARIFY AND ENERGISE

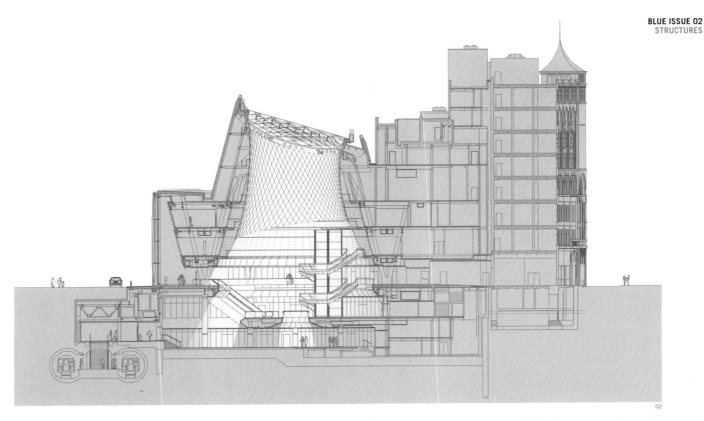

aiming for. A single load leads to a single 'kink' at the point of action, whereas linear loads cause a continuous curve in the structure. The bigger the 'sag' in the cable or the rise of the arch, the smaller the forces are, due to these loading assumptions. So formfinding in this case would lead to a kink or a curve respectively, with a resultant sag that is an acceptable element.

The exercise of formfinding becomes more complicated when we consider the fact that during the lifespan of a structure the forces might change and be linear, singular or otherwise unevenly distributed. In allowing for these variations we observe that increasing the sag of the catenary reduces the forces in the cables under linear loading, but magnifies the deformations under unsymmetrical loading. A conflict of goals becomes apparent, and it appears that structural formfinding comes down to an engineering judgment, the ability to define an optimal balance between several performance parameters of a structure.

Cables are only capable of taking tension forces, meaning that for reversed loading conditions (causing compression forces) a cable would go slack

and the system would fail. This can be mitigated by pre-stressing the cable initially with a tension force which is higher than the expected compression force due to the reversed loading. This means that reversed loading only reduces the initial tension force, without making the cable go slack.

The pre-stress can be introduced by means of weight balancing the reversed loading, which could appear counterintuitive with respect to producing a lightweight structure. The alternative option available to pre-stress a cable is to introduce another cable with a reversed shape. Cable arrangements like this can be pre-stressed against each other and catenaries are even able to have different curvatures leading to different forces in the opposite cables to account for equilibrium.

Both structures mentioned in this essay are by no means simple catenaries but double-curved cable-nets. The intriguing fact about double-curved structures is that they act in three dimensions and if the designers understand the need to make effective use of all three dimensions, these structures become very light and efficient.

01 **VIEW FROM BELOW OF THE CABLE-NET REFLECTOR AND OCULUS AT FULTON STREET TRANSIT CENTER**
02 **SECTIONAL DIAGRAM SHOWING NATURAL LIGHT BEING BROUGHT DOWN TO THE PLATFORM LEVEL**

Besides satisfying the architectural and functional requirements, the geometry of the cable-net must be in equilibrium without slack cables. Therefore, as described above for catenaries, it is imperative for a cable-net to create a surface with negative Gaussian curvature. Pre-stress in one cable direction is balanced and maintained by the pre-stress in the other direction with opposite curvature. The degree of curvature determines the force in the cables and therefore that the required support structure at the net's boundary can be analysed.

A close co-operation between Grimshaw and Schlaich Bergermann and Partners on the Coney Island Center and also with James Carpenter Associates in the case of the Fulton Street reflector was necessary from the beginning of the design process to help clarify the approximate shape, the cable layout and the anticipated cladding of the cable-net to estimate acceptable deformations.

During the long and occasionally difficult design development of the Fulton Street Transit Center project, the only element that remained the same throughout was our commitment to bring natural light down onto the subway platforms and to use this light as both a symbol and a signal; an easily recognisable representation of the light-filled space within which would help to organise and facilitate pedestrian movements within this important transit hub.

Natural light was recognised as an imperative component of the design in terms of serving to clarify and energise a maze of diverse subway lines, street entrances, and underground corridors in one of the busiest transportation hubs found in New York City.

After extensive studies and several iterations, the early ideas including a roof with several 'scoops' or that of an evenly light-transmitting plane over the retail pavilion were abandoned in favour of a single element that would act as a beacon of light over the large void created in the street level of the pavilion.

The first iteration of this dome was a complex grid shell leaning to the north – capturing the light that escaped the neighbouring tall buildings – a structure that worked in compression but that also needed a complex geometry due to its required performance. The initial cost assessments were quite alarming and the design team was required to revisit the concept.

03

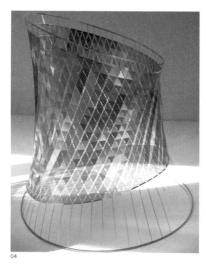

04

03 THE PARASOL WORKS AS A LIGHT FILTER ORIENTED TO REFLECT AND MAXIMISE NATURAL LIGHT THOUGH THE FULTON STREET OCULUS
04 MODEL OF THE CABLE NET MADE WITH THE ACTUAL ALUNOD™ MATERIAL
05 VIEW OF THE PLATFORM LEVEL FROM STREET LEVEL

05

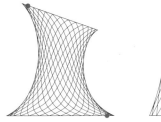

06

06   SMALL LOADS IN THE CABLE NET
      ALLOWED MANIPULATION OF
      CABLE NET CURVATURE TO
      MAXIMISE LIGHT REFLECTION AND
      LIMIT PANEL SIZE VARIATIONS
07   CONCEPT DIAGRAM OF MAJOR
      PROJECT GOALS AND
      COMPONENTS

07

After another series of studies we arrived at a simple but cost effective concept: detach the external cladding from the reflector structure itself.

An easier-to-build circular frustum (the portion of a solid which lies between two parallel planes that cut it) could be built based on elements working in compression and could hang a lighter element, an element whose shape could be manipulated through the use of more efficient tensioned cables.

After studies performed by optics specialist David Norris from James Carpenter's office (the reflector element of the Fulton Street Transit Centre project is part of the Metropolitan Transit Authority 'Arts for Transit' program) pointed towards a hyperbolic paraboloid as the basic shape. A form like this can be produced by diagonally running cables between circular edges. The degree of contraction in the middle is governed by the horizontal offset of the cable attachments between an upper and a lower ring. The more it contracts, the bigger the effective curvature in the surface and the lower the forces in the cables. Unfortunately, this increase in offset results (after bringing it into equilibrium structurally) in very different mesh sizes and an inefficient s-shaped run of a singular cable.

As the loads on the net are quite low and the adjacent structures comparatively stiff, a shape with reduced curvature and slightly increased pre-stress was eventually chosen. This means we end up with more regular sized panels of the Alunod™ cladding, meaning a more consistent overall performance than could have been achieved using the more curved design. Additionally, this is also a much preferred solution with regards to the functional requirement of light deflection.

Coney Island has historically been associated with innovation – many of these innovations being of a novelty or leisure nature – so we consider there to be no better place suited for the erection and celebration of a structure based on its own intrinsic performance requirements. A structure that, like carnival rides such as the Parachute Jump or the Cyclone roller coaster, has been developed based solely on its function and rejoices in exploring the expressive energy that comes from this pure design driver.

Based on the required audience capacity for the covered seating area being set at 5,000 people, – and climatological data analysis of rain events, rain droplet size, wind velocity and occurrence – a canopy of 90 x 85 m / 300 x 279 ft emerged. The principle of designing the cables in a saddle shape/spoked-wheel geometry provided the required free span as well as the efficiency required for a free span within a large surface roof area 20,000 sq m / 65,000 sq ft.

The client on the project, Brooklyn Borough President Marty Markowitz, who harboured memories of weekends spent amongst the magical amusements of the Coney Island of old, immediately embraced the suggested structure, one that had the lightness of the fabric in a parachute while being evocative of the curves of the Cyclone. A new symbolic structure for Coney Island was born.

The 'ring' roof acts according to the principles of a spoked bicycle wheel. An outer compression ring is balanced by means of radial spokes with an inner 'hub' or tension ring. The system is very efficient because the pre-stress does not increase the support forces due to the fact that it is balanced within the compression ring. One of the main structural targets in ensuring a lightweight structure is to avoid bending moments. For 'ring' roofs, this requires a careful alignment of the cable forces and the shape of the compression ring in plan.

A real bicycle wheel is only loaded in plane whereas a ring roof is mainly loaded out-of-plane. This requires the spreading of the spokes out-of-plane in order to stiffen the structure. The second cable layer needs a similar anchorage to the first, which often leads to a second parallel compression ring. This results in a system consisting of radially arranged cable trusses anchored in the hub and in

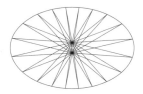

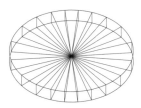

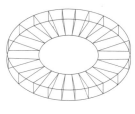

08

10

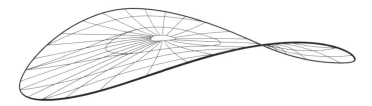

09

THE STRUCTURE HAS THE LIGHTNESS OF THE FABRIC IN A PARACHUTE WHILE BEING EVOCATIVE OF THE CURVES OF THE CYCLONE

08 DIAGRAM OF THE SPOKED
    WHEEL AND INNER HUB
09 THE PARABOLOID SHAPE GIVES
    THE REQUIRED STIFFNESS TO A
    SINGLE CABLE SYSTEM
10 CGI AERIAL VIEW FROM THE
    NORTHEAST
11 CGI VIEW WITHIN THE
    AMPHITHEATRE

11

the compression ring. The horizontal reaction forces are balanced inside these rings.

On the Coney Island Center project, the second cable layer was not desired or ideal, similarly, a planar single layer cable-net would not have been sufficiently stable, which brought us to the conclusion that we should incorporate the third dimension in the design. By creating a double-curved surface, made possible by undulating the compression ring, we were able to negate the need for cable trusses as they are no longer necessary due to the fact that the rigidity of the system is no longer generated from the vertical curvature of the compression ring, and therefore we are left with the final three dimensional curvature of cable-net.

In principle, the cable arrangement within the ring could be radial or rectangular. Investigations with these geometries showed that with radial arrangements the behaviour of the roof structure was more balanced due to the ring cables being able to distribute forces more evenly throughout the structure.

Due to the fact that local deflection has the potential to cause ponding problems in a tensile structure, it was decided that the radial arrangement was preferable. However, the small curvature in parts of the ring and the extreme loading conditions made it necessary to create a hybrid system by opening up part of the cable rings and connecting them directly to the compression ring.

The undulated shape of the compression ring also provided the opportunity to clear the back-of-house-areas as well as enabling the inclusion of a column-free opening towards the lawn seating area. A bending free-compression ring is

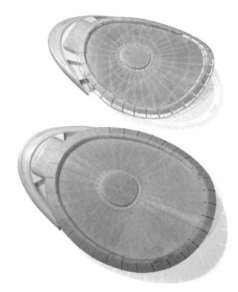

13

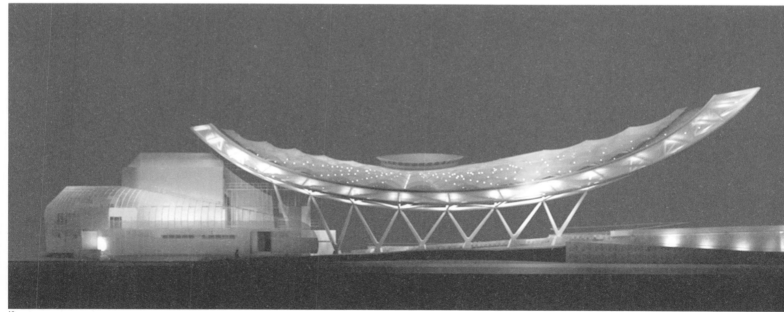

12

14

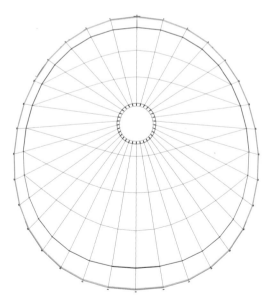

15

practically impossible within these support conditions, however, and providing increased stiffness at the horizontal axis because of the support conditions led to a disproportionate increase of the undesired movements at the vertical axis due to the pre-stress of the cable-net. This issue was mitigated by changing the shape of the ring and by creating a three-chord truss with varying distances between the chords, thereby providing varying levels of rigidity and providing the ability to emphasise the direction where the firmness is most needed.

In summary, both structures – the Fulton Street Transit Center reflector and the Coney Island Center roof – a developmental design process was what led to the final design solution. There was no preconceived form or idealised plan, and only by means of a constant back and forth between the design team, expressing its concerns and explaining the opportunities from the perspective of each discipline, was it possible to come to the final solutions, solutions that incorporate all the requirements of the project stakeholders as well as achieving the most efficient and beautiful structural solution.

If 'efficiency' can be described as the minimum use of resources used to achieve maximum performance, both the Fulton Street and Coney Island project solutions can be described as very efficient structural systems and architectural solutions. It should finally be noted that the freedom we enjoyed and exercised on these projects was intentionally limited by ourselves to a role of steering the design process and advocating simplicity. by allowing the inherent beauty of these light structures to take shape, we were able to fulfill our client brief and realise our practice and team objectives. **Ⓑ**

12 STUDY MODEL OF THE
    STRUCTURE AT NIGHT
13 MODEL OF ROOF AND BACK OF
    HOUSE AT CONEY ISLAND MADE
    WITH DIMENSION™ 3D PRINTER
14 MODEL OF ROOF (RETRACTABLE
    OPTION) AND BACK OF HOUSE
    AT CONEY ISLAND MADE WITH
    DIMENSION™ 3D PRINTER
15 FINAL HYBRID SPOKED
    WHEEL / RECTANGULAR GRID
    CABLE ARRANGEMENT

Design is not guided by
but by the desire to cre
problems. Good design
world around them. Th
absorb and associate f
any idea and see if it w

the quest for certainty,
ate and to solve
ers are open to the
ey have the ability to
reely, come up with
orks.

Adriaan Beukers, Laboratory for Structures and Materials, Delft University of Technology

The Core at the Eden Project demonstrates how an understanding of natural systems led to a dramatic roof structure. The story of this design challenge is told here by three of Grimshaw's design team.

Eden Project: The Core
Cornwall, UK

CORE VALUES

Jolyon Brewis
Managing Partner

Andrew Thomas
Associate Director

Jerry Tate
Jerry Tate Architects

01

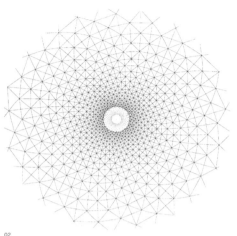

02

03

The Core is a purpose-built education building at the Eden Project in Cornwall. It was conceived to help convey Eden's central message about the relationship between mankind and the natural world around us, with a particular focus on plants. The resulting design connects mathematical formulae, natural systems for efficient growth in plants, and a geometry that resonates throughout the organic and inorganic world.

The defining feature of the building is a roof that spans from a central ring of supports over all of the main spaces within the building, including an exhibition space, classrooms, a cafeteria and offices. Visible from all key areas of the building, this roof offered an opportunity to 'speak' to everyone who passes through. It does so through the incorporation of a geometry found in the system of plant growth known as spiral phyllotaxis, in which a number of spirals radiate in two directions to form a grid. Many plants demonstrate this growth pattern, which accommodates the maximum number of seed heads to grow sequentially in a given area: an example of highly efficient 'packing'.

VISIBLE FROM ALL KEY AREAS OF THE BUILDING THE ROOF OFFERED AN OPPORTUNITY TO 'SPEAK' TO EVERYONE WHO PASSES THROUGH

This geometry was explored with Peter Randall-Page, a sculptor who became an intrinsic part of our design team. With many years of experience in the study and interpretation of natural geometries and forms in his own sculptural work, Peter became an invaluable collaborator, opening our eyes to the possibilities of spiral phyllotaxis in our design. As one of the archetypal natural patterns, we felt that this geometry could form the basis for the roof of the Core in such a way that it could be explained to all visitors, but that it would also communicate more implicitly something of the inherent 'rightness' of a pattern that has evolved over millennia. Early incarnations of our design intuitively used a symmetrical approach to the geometry, with an equal number of spirals in each direction, and this was proving very inefficient in structural terms. Peter helped us to understand the natural occurrences of the pattern, and the strict mathematical rules that underpin it.

Interestingly, this organic pattern relates to a system of proportion used by artists and architects for hundreds of years. Examination of all examples of spiral phyllotaxis in nature reveals that the numbers of spirals radiating clockwise and anti-clockwise are always two consecutive numbers from the Fibonacci numerical sequence. This sequence, first postulated by Leonardo da Pisa (or Fibonacci, as he was nicknamed), is such that the next consecutive number is the sum of the two previous numbers: 0, 1, 1, 2, 3, 5, 8, 13, 21, 34, 55, etc. The ratio between each consecutive pair of numbers tends to 0.618, or 'phi', otherwise known as the Golden Ratio, and informs the 'Golden Section' proportion used by architects from Vitruvius to Le Corbusier and beyond.

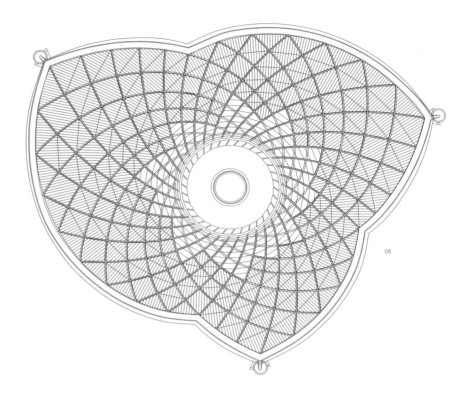

05

04

01 **THE HEAD OF A DAISY,
AN EXAMPLE OF NATURE USING
A PHYLLOTACTIC GEOMETRY
TO 'CLOSE PACK' CELL GROWTH
FROM A CENTRAL POINT**
02 **THE BEGINNING OF OUR
INTERPRETATION OF THE
SPIRAL GRID. STRUCTURAL
EFFICIENCY ONLY CAME
WITH A CLOSER READING OF
NATURALLY OCCURRING SPIRAL
GEOMETRIES**
03 **THE ROOF STRUCTURE FROM
BELOW**
04 **FIBONACCI AND THE GOLDEN
RATIO: THE MATHEMATICAL
BASIS OF A PURE SPIRAL
GEOMETRY**
05 **THE CORE'S ROOF PLAN,
DEMONSTRATING THE
FINAL, ASYMMETRIC SPIRAL
GEOMETRY**

With a more detailed understanding of the pattern, we redesigned our grid, hoping that some of nature's efficiency would also help our roof structure. For the roof of the Core, a geometry was established with a grid of 21 and 34 spirals, developed with Mike Purvis, a structural engineer with SKM. His enthusiasm and technical expertise led to a roof structure that could be efficiently constructed using laminated timber. To our delight Mike's calculations, based on nature's formula, showed that the problem had been solved.

Such a complex geometry led to a whole range of interesting design challenges before the roof could be realised, some of which are described here by Andrew Thomas. The process of sourcing and building the roof is described by Jerry Tate. Whilst the geometry of the roof is described here,

many other stories could be told about the building, including the passive air heating and cooling, the first sustainable certification of the copper roof cladding, and the incorporation of arts and interpretive material within the fabric of the building (not least the installation of Peter Randall-Page's sculpture, 'Seed', at the heart of the building, carrying the same phyllotactic pattern across its surface of undulating granite).

The result of all of this work was a building that fulfilled all of the functional requirements for the Eden Project's educational facility. Just as important has been the incorporation of botanical imagery in a contemporary and meaningful way, in the very structure of the building. This has answered one of the client's key requirements: to take the message of our dependency on plants to a deeper level.

The Collaborative Process Grimshaw and Haring

Take a toroidal surface and project two counter-vailing spiral grids vertically through it: the underlying geometry of the Core's roof is a relatively simple thing. Once the project's resident structural engineer, enthusiast of advanced maths and all-round Renaissance Man, Mike Purvis, had written his 'Phyllotactic Generator' (a piece of software which calculated the precise co-ordinates of our spiral grid), the building geometry could be modelled in three dimensions with no more than a few dozen clicks of the mouse.

Developing the form of the roof's upper surface was much more time-consuming, but still relatively straightforward. Following the biomimetic theme, there was a very clear concept for an array of overlapping 'leaves', echoing the roof's spiral geometry, not unlike the leaves of an artichoke. Through a series of physical models we developed some simple rules around the practicalities of turning a flattened-out artichoke into a water-shedding roof. Coming before the advent of parametric modelling (at least for the author!), the final geometry of the roof could only be developed through individual modelling, testing and adjustment of each roof panel until each 'leaf' obeyed all of these rules.

By the time our Swiss timber specialists, Haring, joined the team, the building geometry was set, along with some quite well-defined proposals for its fabrication. In the months that followed, the relationship between the design team and Haring provided a clear illustration of the value of open collaborative working, as Haring brought their expert knowledge of material performance, fabrication and construction to the team. The apparent simplicity of the process described above belied some areas of significant hidden complexity, once the limitations of technology – and budget – were understood fully. Responsible for the full extent of the building's timber structure and envelope, Haring contributed significant 'Eureka' moments

06

THE END RESULT WAS A REMARKABLY LIGHT, MONOCOQUE STRUCTURE FOR THE ROOF PANELS

throughout the detail design; however, one moment, detailed below, is particularly memorable.

An immediate consequence of selecting two dissimilar spiral geometries for the building grid is that each of the cells defined by that grid is unique. While the team were quick to understand the inefficiency inherent in fabricating 190 unique roof panels, each double-curved and twisting in plane, we knew that the expression of each unique 'leaf' on the roof was fundamental to the building concept. In this case it was Haring who identified an elegant

06 THE SURFACE OF THE ROOF WAS TREATED AS A SERIES OF COPPER 'LEAVES'. WHERE DAYLIGHT WAS REQUIRED WITHIN, THE LEAVES OPENED TO CREATE ROOF LIGHTS

07 WHILST ALL INDIVIDUAL CELLS ARE UNIQUE, EACH RADIAL RIBBON HAS AN IDENTICAL BASE GEOMETRY. UNDERSTANDING THIS WAS KEY TO EFFICIENT PRE-FABRICATION OF THE ROOF

07

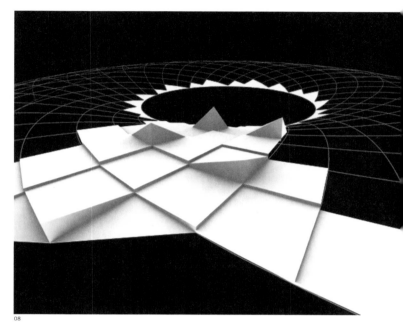

08

08 MODELLING THE ROOF CELL-BY-
CELL WAS KEY TO GENERATING,
AND THEN TESTING, THE ROOF
GEOMETRY

09 OUTPUT FROM THE
'PHYLLOTACTIC GENERATOR'
DEFINED THE PRECISE CO-
ORDINATES OF OUR
SPIRAL GRID

solution: whilst each individual cell may be unique, the roof panels could equally well be fabricated as a series of spiral ribbons, each of which would be identical. As the dialogue continued, we discovered further benefits in this strategy: both the building services and roof drainage worked most efficiently in a simple radial direction and provision for these elements could now be pre-fabricated into the roof panels in the factory.

As for the clear expression of the individual 'leaves', this could be achieved by simply extending the edge plates of the ribbons to follow the stepped profile required. The end result was a remarkably light, monocoque structure for the roof panels, pre-fabricated entirely from engineered timber board and transported in large modules to the Eden site.

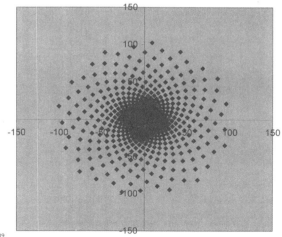

09

Sourcing a Complex Timber Roof

One of the great joys of designing a large span timber gridshell roof is meeting the amazing people involved in the design, supply and manufacture of the structure. At the time of undertaking development of the roof for the Core, the timber structure expertise in the UK was more limited than today, so we looked for specialists on the continent who could help us deliver the roof in a sustainable manner. This initial 'contractor hunt' involved a madcap tour by train and bus around southern Germany, Austria and Switzerland with Eden, SKM Anthony Hunts, Davis Langdon and McAlpine JV. After a series of disappointing meetings we eventually met Chris Haring of Haring AG, near Basel, who (to our slight disbelief) declared that our proposed roof would be 'no problem'; to prove it, he showed us an incredible double-curved gluelam structure he had completed at a nearby public baths. From this initial meeting we started a very fruitful design dialogue, which also provided us with an insight into Swiss methods of manufacture.

Haring AG, a family company, operates within a network of similar companies in their local region. Although not formally linked, they all have an understanding in terms of each other's capabilities, timescales and methods. They also demonstrate a deep sense of social commitment with their relationship to the community and the environment. Sometimes this results in astounding feats unheard of in the UK; for example Haring, in co-operation with other companies, was capable of building high quality affordable housing extremely quickly with a house taking approximately one day to assemble on site (from pre-fabricated components).

One of our more interesting visits was inspecting the supply chain for the Core's timber structure, from timber supply to the CNC milling. Meeting the foresters was fantastic; Switzerland produces approximately 3 million tonnes of timber per annum, but only has a domestic requirement of 1 million tonnes meaning that the surplus needs

10

THE TIMBER WASTE WAS FED IN TO A DISTRICT HEATING SYSTEM THAT HEATED BOTH THE FACTORY AND THE SURROUNDING VILLAGE

11   12

10 THE TIMBER STRUCTURE IN ITS COMPLETE STATE
11 CAREFUL STEWARDSHIP OF THE FOREST WAS MANAGED BY THE INDIVIDUAL IDENTIFICATION AND 'PLUCKING' OF TREES FOR USE IN THE PROJECT
12 A GLUELAM ROOF BEAM BEFORE ITS FINAL FINISH: TRAPEZOIDAL IN SECTION, DOUBLE-CURVED AND TWISTING IN PLANE
13 FIXING THE BEAM CURVATURES IN THE HARING FACTORY REQUIRED THE USE OF A TRIPLE AXIS JIG
14 BEAMS WERE CUT DOWN INTO THEIR LENGTHS FOR TRANSPORTATION BEFORE FINAL FINISHING WAS UNDERTAKEN

to be exported. Instead of felling large sections of the forest, trees are felled with a machine which literally 'plucks' them individually from the ground and strips them immediately with no detrimental effect on the surrounding trees. This allows the forest to be thinned as required, without a blanket removal program. The sawmill where the timber was processed was fastidious in using every part of the tree, including the timber waste which was fed in to a district heating system that not only heated the factory but the surrounding village as well! At Haring's factory, computer-controlled hydraulic jigs enabled the complex geometry of the roof to be translated into the double-curved laminated beams. The highlight for me, however, was the CNC milling factory where the timber components were milled to within a 1mm tolerance, before being transported to the UK and assembled on site. All of these stages of manufacture were performed at separate companies, yet all were within half an hour of each other (and generally could be reached by train, with the exception of the forest).

Timber frame manufacture in the UK is now expanding at an exponential rate to cope with our increasing demands for sustainable, low-carbon buildings. One of my most heartfelt desires is that we achieve the level of craftsmanship and social responsibility I witnessed in action in the Swiss industry. Ⓑ

Blue is a CarbonNeutral Publication. CO_2 emissions to design, print and deliver the book have been measured using a carbon calculator and 100% offset by purchasing carbon credits for reductions in greenhouse emissions made at another location, such as wind farms which create renewable energy and reduce the need for fossil-fuel powered energy.

Printed by Beacon Press, a CarbonNeutral® company, using their **pureprint** environmental print technology committed to reducing the impact of printing on the environment, registered to environmental management systems ISO14001 and EMAS.

100% of the electricity used to print this book is generated from renewable sources, only vegetable based inks were used in the production, 95% of the press cleaning solvents used have been recycled and 98% of any dry waste associated with this product has been recycled and diverted from landfill.

The paper is Think4 White, containing 50% recycled post consumer fibre and material sourced from responsibly managed forests certified in accordance with the FSC (Forest Stewardship Council). Paper manufactured at an ISO14001 accredited mill.

pure**print**

EMAS
VERIFIED
ENVIRONMENTAL
MANAGEMENT
REG. NO. UK – S – 0000011

FSC
Mixed Sources
Product group from well-managed
forests, controlled sources and
recycled wood or fiber

Cert no. SGS-COC-0620
www.fsc.org
© 1996 Forest Stewardship Council

Editor
Andrew Whalley

Graphic design / production
Neil Nisbet

Copywriting / proofreading
Taya Brendle
Kelly Young

Research
Jenny Dudgeon
Chi Ying Shen

Production assistants
Allison Dolegowski
Freya Klein

© **GRIMSHAW** 2010

ISBN: 978–0–9825875–0–8

GRIMSHAW

57 Clerkenwell Road
London
EC1M 5NG
UK

T +44 (0)20 7291 4141
F +44 (0)20 7291 4194

100 Reade Street
New York
NY 10013
USA

T +1 212 791 2501
F +1 212 791 2173

494 LaTrobe Street
Melbourne
VIC 3000
Australia

T +61 (0)3 9321 2600
F +61(0)3 9321 2611

info@grimshaw-architects.com
www.grimshaw-architects.com